YORK NOTE

York Notes Rapid Revision

A Christmas Carol

AQA GCSE English Literature

Written by Lyn Lockwood

YORK PRESS
322 Old Brompton Road, London SW5 9JH

PEARSON EDUCATION LIMITED
80 Strand, London,
WC2R 0RL, United Kingdom
Associated companies, branches and representatives throughout the world

10 9 8 7 6 5 4 3 2 1

ISBN 978–1–2922–7088–3

Phototypeset by Ken Vail Graphic Design
Printed in Slovakia

Image credits:
GL Archive/Alamy for page 4 top / Julia700702/Shutterstock for page 6 top and page 26 top / Josef Hanus/Shutterstock for page 8 top, page 32 top and page 46 bottom / simon evans/Alamy for page 10 top / Cranach/Shutterstock for page 12 top and page 32 bottom / Pristine Images/© iStock for page 14 middle / Chantal de Bruijne/Shutterstock for page 16 middle / lou armor/Shutterstock for page 20 middle / Alexander Raths/Shutterstock for page 22 middle / Gilmanshin/Shutterstock for page 24 top / Leigh Prather/Shutterstock for page 28 bottom / TCD/Prod.DB/Alamy for page 30 top and page 44 top/ Patrick LaCroix/Alamy for page 34 top and page 58 bottom / haeton/Shutterstock for page 36 top / azulox/© iStock for page 36 middle / Loop Images Ltd/Alamy for page 38 top and page 52 bottom/ Kateryna Yakoylieva/Shutterstock for page 38 bottom and page 52 top / Oksana Schmidt/Shutterstock for page 42 bottom / Ozornina/Shutterstock for page 48 top / Podolnava Elena/Shutterstock for page 50 top / Atlantisg/Shutterstock for page 56 middle / marilyna/© iStock for page 60 bottom

CONTENTS

INTRODUCTION Who was Charles Dickens?

Three key things about Charles Dickens

1. Dickens was born in 1812 and had a difficult early life due to his father's financial problems.
2. Dickens wrote over twenty books including **novels**, short stories and non-fiction.
3. Dickens was much loved in his lifetime and he travelled the country reading his books to packed halls.

What happened in Dickens's early life?

- He was born in Portsmouth and initially was sent to school.
- At the age of twelve, Dickens was forced to work in a blacking factory to help to support his family who were living in the debtor's prison with his father.
- Dickens became a journalist, which gave him such an eye for detail.

Why did he write *A Christmas Carol*?

- Dickens read a government report about child poverty in 1843 and was appalled. In response, he decided to write a story to 'strike a sledgehammer blow' on behalf of poor children.
- Dickens argued that employers, like Scrooge, should be held responsible for ensuring their workers had reasonable conditions.
- His description of Martha Cratchit working long hours for little pay was typical of the way young people were forced to live.

What was the response to *A Christmas Carol*?

- Most reviewers and readers praised it highly both for its characters and its powerful message.
- Fellow novelist William M. Thackeray suggested that people rush out 'and purchase five thousand more copies'.
- Ironically, Dickens was criticised for the high cost of the book, which was expensively bound and illustrated. Later editions were cheaper and more affordable for ordinary families.

Stave One
- It's Christmas Eve, and miserly Scrooge is introduced at work.
- He is visited by nephew Fred and charity collectors whom he rejects.
- Back at Scrooge's home, Marley's Ghost appears.
- Scrooge is told he'll be visited by Three Spirits to teach him to amend his ways.

Stave Two
- The first Christmas Ghost arrives at 1 a.m.
- The Ghost of Christmas Past changes shape, looking old and young.
- Scrooge is shown himself as a child and young man by the Ghost.
- Scrooge sees how his love of money began to develop.

Stave Four
- Scrooge is next visited by the Ghost of Christmas Yet to Come.
- It shows Scrooge people's reactions to an unnamed dead man.
- Scrooge is horrified to see that Tiny Tim has died.
- Scrooge sees his own grave and vows to change.

Stave Three
- Scrooge is visited by the Ghost of Christmas Present.
- The Ghost shows Scrooge Christmas celebrations across the country.
- Scrooge learns Tiny Tim will die if he does not change.
- The Ghost reveals the figures of Ignorance and Want beneath his robes.

Stave Five
- Scrooge wakes up on a sunny Christmas Day morning.
- He realises that he now has a second chance and is delighted.
- Scrooge sends a huge turkey to the Cratchits.
- He goes on to live a happy and generous life.

Five key things about Stave One

This Stave introduces us to Scrooge and describes his encounter with Marley's Ghost:

1. We learn that Scrooge is the **sole surviving partner** of a successful business in the centre of **London**.

2. **Scrooge's mean character and hatred** of everyone around him are explored in detail.

3. Despite the **opportunities to be generous** presented by Christmas, Scrooge remains mean and unpleasant.

4. Marley's Ghost and his punishment introduce the themes of **responsibility** towards others, **greed and avarice** and a person's **ability to change**.

5. Dickens wants to keep to the style of the ghost story **genre**, so he is concerned that we believe in the existence of the ghosts in the story.

What happens when we first meet Scrooge?

- The Stave begins with a description of Marley's cheaply arranged funeral, at which Scrooge made an **'undoubted bargain'**.

- At his office, Scrooge is described as **'tight-fisted'** and **'hard and sharp as flint'** with a **'grating'** voice and a **'cold'** manner.

- Scrooge refuses to spend Christmas with his nephew Fred, threatens to sack his employee Bob Cratchit, will not donate money to the charity collectors, saying the poor can live in **'prisons'** and frightens a carol singer.

What happens when Marley's Ghost appears?

- As Scrooge arrives home, Marley's Ghost appears as a face in the doorknocker, and then makes Scrooge's bells ring before he enters the room.

- Marley explains that the chains he drags behind him were **'forged in life'** and that Scrooge has an even longer chain, reflecting Scrooge's longer life of avarice and miserliness.

- Marley warns Scrooge that he has a chance to change and that **'Three Spirits'** will visit him in order to help him avoid this punishment.

Five key quotations

1. Scrooge separates himself from everyone around him, preferring 'to edge his way along the crowded paths of life'.

2. Scrooge hates Christmas: 'a time for finding yourself a year older, and not an hour richer'.

3. Fred appreciates Christmas as: a time, 'when men and women seem by one consent to open their shut-up hearts freely'.

4. Marley's Ghost on responsibility: 'Mankind was my business'.

5. The regret of the London ghosts: 'they sought to interfere, for good, in human matters and had lost the power for ever'.

Note it!

Although Stave One introduces many serious issues, such as poverty and greed, there are typically Dickensian moments of humour, such as the reflection on the meaning behind the **phrase**, **'dead as a door-nail'**. Dickens's use of humour ensures the reader is always engaged.

Exam focus

How can I write about language?

You can use Stave One to write about the use of language in *A Christmas Carol*.

> Dickens's use of language is shown by the way that he describes Scrooge. His description of Scrooge as preferring to, 'edge his way along the crowded paths of life' is both literal and metaphorical. The verb 'edge' implies deliberate movement, keeping far away from anyone. Scrooge is also metaphorically distanced as he appears to have no empathy for other people, preferring to distance himself from all around him.

Topic sentence

Uses language terminology

Explains significance of quotation

Makes wider links

Now you try!

Finish this paragraph about attitudes towards Christmas in Stave One. Use one of the quotations from the list.

Fred and Scrooge have very different attitudes towards Christmas. Fred's attitude is positive ....

My progress   Needs more work ☐   Getting there ☐   Sorted! ☐

PLOT AND STRUCTURE Stave Two

Five key things about Stave Two

This Stave introduces us to the first Ghost and shows us Scrooge's childhood:

1. We meet the **Ghost of Christmas Past** who appears to flicker and change shape, looking like both **a child** and **an old man**.

2. **Scrooge's journey** in understanding who he is and why he needs to **change begins**. This means making Scrooge **confront** all aspects of his life.

3. The Spirit shows Scrooge his **school**, and his **sister, Fan**.

4. Scrooge is shown **Fezziwig**, his friendly first **employer**. Scrooge also sees **Belle**, his first love.

5. The **ghost story genre** is further developed as the reader is taken on a **supernatural journey** in time and place.

What happens when the first Ghost appears?

- The Stave begins in Scrooge's bedroom as the clock strikes one o'clock and Scrooge comes **'face to face'** with the **'unearthly visitor'**.
- The Ghost of Christmas Past appears as a changing human shape often with **'no outline visible'**. Scrooge asks for its light to be **'covered'** in his fear.
- The Ghost tells Scrooge he is there for Scrooge's **'welfare'** and takes Scrooge back in time to his school days. Scrooge sees himself as a lonely school boy.

What else does the Ghost show Scrooge?

- The Ghost shows Scrooge his sister, Fan, who we learn was a **'delicate creature'** and died after giving birth to Scrooge's nephew, Fred.
- Scrooge sees himself as a happy young man working for Fezziwig. Scrooge also sees his former sweetheart, Belle, who tells him he is too obsessed with money. Belle breaks off their relationship.
- The Ghost returns Scrooge to his bed. Shocked and **'exhausted'**, Scrooge falls fast asleep.

Five key quotations

1. The Ghost of Christmas Past is angry when Scrooge wants it to go away: 'would you so soon put out, with worldly hands, the light I give?'
2. The **theme** of the supernatural: 'The city had entirely vanished.'
3. Scrooge feels emotions that he cannot understand: 'Why did his cold eye glisten, and his heart leap up as they went past?'
4. The theme of being responsible for others: 'The happiness he gives, is quite as great as if it cost a fortune.' (Scrooge about Fezziwig).
5. Scrooge's greed: 'the master-passion, Gain, engrosses you' (Belle).

Note it!

The Ghost's changing shape makes it look both old and young as it represents all the different people in Scrooge's life and the need for him to change. Its shining light reveals the truth to Scrooge about himself.

Exam focus

How can I write about themes? AO1

You can use Stave Two to write about the theme of responsibility in *A Christmas Carol*.

The theme of responsibility is shown by Fezziwig's treatment of his staff. This causes Scrooge to exclaim, 'The happiness he gives, is quite as great as if it cost a fortune!' Here Scrooge learns that money is not the only key to helping others, and this theme is developed throughout the novel in Scrooge's evolving treatment of his own employee, Bob Cratchit.

Topic sentence makes overall point

Key quotation for theme

Explains significance of quotation

Makes links across the novel

Now you try!

Finish this paragraph about the presentation of Scrooge in Stave Two. Use one of the quotations from the list.

Dickens continues to develop the presentation of character in Stave Two. An important aspect of .... character is revealed when ....

Five key things about Stave Three

This Stave introduces the second Ghost and shows us a variety of Christmas scenes:

1. We meet the **Ghost of Christmas Present** – the second of the Three Spirits who are due to visit Scrooge.

2. This Ghost's role is to make Scrooge understand the **importance of Christmas** for both rich and poor, people near and far, family and strangers.

3. The **'gigantic' Ghost represents all the wealth and generosity** that can be found at Christmas, but he is also there to remind Scrooge that it is equally important to be kind to each other.

4. The visit to the Cratchit house shows Scrooge beginning to feel **empathy** for the family's struggles.

5. The Stave ends with the terrifying Children **'Ignorance and Want'** who remind Scrooge, and the reader, of the book's **moral message**. The children **symbolise** Dickens's passionate belief in educating and helping the poor.

What happens when the Ghost visits Scrooge?

- The Ghost of Christmas Present arrives surrounded by Christmas food. The Ghost shows Scrooge 'jovial' shoppers and 'delicious' Christmas treats.

- Scrooge watches how the Cratchits enjoy Christmas. The Ghost warns Scrooge that Tiny Tim may die if the family are not helped.

- The Ghost takes Scrooge to a coal miner's home, a ship and even a lighthouse, to remind Scrooge that the Christmas spirit can exist anywhere.

What happens at the end of Stave Three?

- Scrooge and the Ghost visit Fred's house where they are celebrating Christmas.

- Scrooge hears Fred's wife say, **'I have no patience with him'**, as they discuss Scrooge's mean behaviour.

- The Stave ends with the shocking image of the withered and monstrous children **'Ignorance and Want'** who represent the dangers of poverty.

Five key quotations

1. The Victorian Christmas: 'Holly, mistletoe, red berries, ivy, turkeys, geese, game, poultry ….'
2. The Cratchits enjoy their Christmas, despite their poverty: 'Bob said he didn't believe there ever was such a goose cooked.'
3. The **theme** of empathy: 'Oh no, kind Spirit! say he will be spared!' (Scrooge about Tiny Tim).
4. The feelings of the Cratchit family about Scrooge: 'Scrooge was the Ogre of the family.'
5. Ignorance and Want: 'wretched, abject, frightful, hideous, miserable'.

Note it!

Dickens uses language techniques to describe the Victorian Christmas, such as the **personification** of Spanish Onions as **'winking from their shelves'** and chestnuts **'like the waistcoats of jolly old gentleman'**, and active **verbs** **'clashing'**, **'tumbled'** and **'jostled'** to convey excitement.

Exam focus

How can I write about character?

You can use Stave Three to explore the characters of the Cratchit family.

> Dickens presents the importance of being kind at Christmas. The Cratchit family's appreciation of their meagre dinner, 'Bob said he didn't believe there ever was such a goose cooked', represents that belief. This is juxtaposed with Mrs Cratchit's description of Scrooge as 'stingy'. The pitiful Tiny Tim forces Scrooge to be reminded of his own past cruelty and Scrooge's belief that if the poor died it would 'decrease the surplus population'.

Topic sentence makes overall point

Quotation supports opening sentence

Describes a language technique

Makes wider links across the novel

Now you try!

Finish this paragraph about the presentation of poverty in Stave Three. Use one of the quotations from the list.

> Another function of Stave Three is to explore the effects of poverty. Dickens presents the children 'Ignorance and Want' that live.............................

Five key things about Stave Four

In this Stave we meet the **Ghost of Christmas Yet to Come** and Scrooge sees his possible future:

1. This is the **most frightening** of all the Ghosts. Scrooge bends **'down upon his knee'** in fear of the Ghost and **pays close attention** to what he is shown.

2. Scrooge learns the **effect of living a greedy and unkind life** as he sees that people who knew him either do not care that he has died or are actually happy.

3. **The death of Tiny Tim**, in contrast, shows a family who are devastated by their grief and sadness and is a **powerful moment** in the **novel**.

4. Scrooge is shown his own grave which is the **climax** of the Ghosts' visits.

5. The Stave ends with **Scrooge's final chance to change** and gain future happiness.

What does the Ghost first show Scrooge?

- The Ghost of Christmas Yet to Come appears. It does not speak to Scrooge. The Ghost shows him a number of different people talking about a man who has died.

- These include business people who knew the man, thieves who stole from him and a young couple who owed the man rent. None of them cares that the man has died.

- Scrooge refuses to look at the face of the dead man.

What does the Ghost finally show Scrooge?

- Scrooge watches the Cratchits mourning the death of Tiny Tim.

- The Ghost also shows Scrooge his office with someone he does not recognise working there.

- The Ghost takes Scrooge to a graveyard and shows him a gravestone that has Scrooge's name on it. The Ghost confirms that it was Scrooge the people were talking about earlier in the Stave. Begging for a second chance, Scrooge agrees to change and become a better person.

Five key quotations

1. People joke about Scrooge's death: 'It's likely to be a very cheap funeral.'
2. The **theme** of poverty and its link to crime: 'the whole quarter reeked with crime, with filth, with misery'.
3. Scrooge's isolation: 'He frightened every one away from him when he was alive, to profit us when he was dead!'
4. Strong family ties and emotions: '"My little, little child!" cried Bob. "My little child!"'
5. Change: 'Assure me that I yet may change these shadows you have shown me, by an altered life!'

Note it!

The Ghosts grow increasingly more frightening and more powerful as the story progresses. The first **symbolises** childhood and growth, the second **personifies** the spirit of Christmas, but the last Ghost is clearly symbolic of Death itself. It is therefore unsurprising that this silent Ghost wears a **'deep black garment'**.

Exam focus

How can I write about form? AO2

You can use Stave Four to write about the **form** of *A Christmas Carol* both as a ghost story and a morality tale.

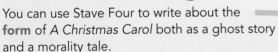

As Scrooge looks to the Ghost to 'assure' him that he can change this terrifying future, the verb 'assure' reflects Scrooge's desperation to show he has understood the Ghost's moral lesson of kindness and generosity. The noun 'shadows' signifies the future events that Scrooge has been shown by the supernatural forces, and is typical of the vocabulary of a book written in the form of a ghost story, alongside words such as 'Phantom', 'Spirit' and 'Spectre'.

- Uses language terminology
- Topic defined as explanation of moral message
- Explains significance of quotation
- Makes wider links to other key vocabulary

Now you try!

Finish this paragraph about the presentation of emotion. Use one of the quotations from the list.

Stave Four presents different characters' thoughts and feelings about each other. An important aspect of strong emotion is explored when . . . .

Five key things about Stave Five

In this Stave we see how Scrooge has finally changed:

1. This Stave **contrasts** with the rest of the **novel** in many ways. It is **funny** and full of sunlight and **happiness**, whereas so far the **mood** has been full of fear and misery.

2. Dickens was a **comic writer** and this Stave contains many **funny images** such as Scrooge struggling to put on his stockings.

3. Scrooge's **first acts of kindness** are anonymous. Scrooge realises **generosity** should not require thanks or praise.

4. Scrooge is now **realistic** about people's attitudes towards him. He admits to the charity collector that the name 'Scrooge' may not **'be pleasant'** to him. Scrooge also understands that some **'people laughed to see the alteration in him'** but accepts this.

5. Tiny Tim's line **'God bless Us, Every One!'** reminds us of the novel's **Christian message** and that Dickens's London was a Christian society.

What happens on Christmas Day?

- Scrooge wakes up on a sunny Christmas Day and is full of life and laughter. Scrooge knows this is his chance to put everything right.

- Scrooge sends a huge **'prize Turkey'** to the Cratchits and arranges to donate a large amount of money to charity, including **'many back-payments'**.

- Scrooge visits Fred. Scrooge's Christmas Day with his family is filled with **'won-der-ful happiness!'**

What happens after Christmas Day?

- On Boxing Day, Scrooge pretends to tell Bob Cratchit off for arriving late at the office. Scrooge quickly reveals he is joking.

- Scrooge increases Bob's pay and makes the office a much nicer place, crying **'Make up the fires'**.

- We learn that Scrooge becomes a **'second father'** to Tiny Tim and a good friend to people across the city.

Five key quotations

1. Brightness on Christmas Day: 'No fog, no mist; clear, bright, jovial, stirring, cold'.
2. Scrooge's newfound friendliness: he 'patted children on the head, and questioned beggars'.
3. Scrooge is welcomed back to the family: 'He was at home in five minutes. Nothing could be heartier.'
4. Scrooge's love for Tiny Tim: 'to tiny Tim, who did NOT die, he was a second father.'
5. The significance of Christmas to the reformed Scrooge: 'he knew how to keep Christmas well'.

Note it!

Dickens is a humorous writer although we may not always find his writing funny today. Try to recognise and understand his jokes. For example, in Stave Five, Dickens creates humour from Scrooge **'frisking'** the saucepan around and Scrooge greeting the Christmas turkey: **'Here's the Turkey. Hallo! Whoop!'**

Exam focus

How can I write about structure?

You can use Stave Five to write about the structure of *A Christmas Carol*, as it is the end of the story.

> Stave Five provides a resolution to the novel and inverts (or turns upside down) Scrooge's behaviour. Dickens portrays Scrooge putting right his earlier wrongs by donating money to charity and even patting the doorknocker that once terrified him. Scrooge interacts with people on the street, 'patted children on the head, and questioned beggars' in contrast with the Scrooge in Stave One who avoids crowds at all costs.

Uses sophisticated vocabulary

Provides evidence for opening topic sentence

Gives relevant quotation

Links to the start of novel

Now you try!

Finish this paragraph about the setting in Stave Five. Use one of the quotations from the list.

Dickens deliberately changes the weather in Stave Five to reflect the change in Scrooge. The wintry weather is now described as ....

My progress Needs more work ☐ Getting there ☐ Sorted! ☐

Five key things about Dickens's use of form and structure

1. *A Christmas Carol* is written as a **novella** or short novel.
2. It is **divided** into five chapters, or 'Staves'.
3. The structure involves many **changes in time and place**.
4. The novella is written in the **form** of a **ghost story**, but it is also **a comedy and a morality tale**.
5. The novella has a **narrator** who sometimes comments on the action and characters.

What is the form of *A Christmas Carol*?

- The ghost story form allows Dickens to make the story both frightening but also to use the supernatural to travel in time and place.

- The form of a short novel means that the story could be read aloud and shared easily.

- The story is also in the **genre** of a morality tale. Such tales help readers to think about their own lives and how they could change for the better, like Scrooge.

- Dickens employs the form of social commentary, using the story's narrator to criticise Victorian society and its attitudes towards the poor.

How does Dickens structure *A Christmas Carol*?

- Dickens divides the novella into five 'Staves' which reminds the reader of lines of music, like a 'carol' to be shared at Christmas.

- The narrator gives us extra information about the characters and situations, such as the weather, to add realism to the story.

- Each Ghost contributes to a new stage in the **plot** and builds tension for the reader.

- The **climax** of the plot comes when Scrooge sees his own gravestone. This is Scrooge's **epiphany**, which is a moment of his life when he comes to a new understanding of the world.

- The **resolution** of the plot is Scrooge's change in character.

Five key quotations

1. Narrative **voice**: 'Scrooge and he were partners for I don't know how many years.'
2. Changes in place and time: 'The Spirit touched him on the arm, and pointed to his younger self'.
3. The traditional structure of a morality tale: 'Once upon a time ....'
4. Developing action through the Ghosts' visits: '"You will be haunted," resumed the Ghost, "by Three Spirits."'
5. The plot's resolution: 'I will honour Christmas in my heart and try to keep it all the year.'

Note it!

Dickens wrote a **preface** to the novella that says he hopes it raises a **'Ghost of an Idea'** in the reader. This pun on the word 'Ghost' makes it clear that he wanted the story to make people think about their own behaviour.

Exam focus

How can I write about Dickens's use of form and structure? (AO2)

You can discuss the **genre** of A Christmas Carol.

Dickens uses the form of a ghost story to develop ideas and to provide a clear structure. Marley's ghost personifies the consequences of greed and furthermore begins the action, when he tells Scrooge 'You will be haunted ... by Three Spirits.' This initiates the structure of the three visits which grow increasingly serious and frightening, ending in the climactic moment when Scrooge sees his own grave.

| Topic sentence about structure |
| Quotation providing evidence |
| Describes effect of structure |
| Use of key term |

Now you try!

Finish this paragraph about the narrative voice. Use one of the quotations from the list.

Dickens uses a clear narrative voice to imply that the story is being read out loud to us. The narrative voice sometimes makes first-person comments, such as ....

1. Look at this ideas map representing Stave One. Is there anything else you could add?

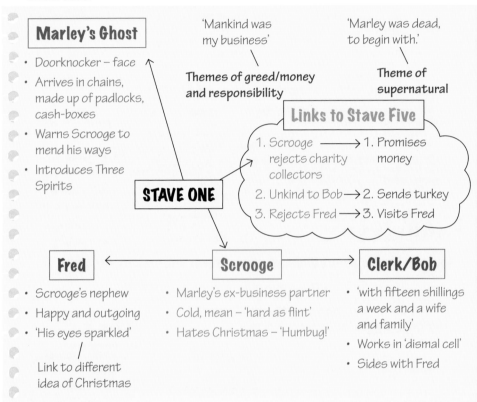

2. Create your own ideas map for one of the other Staves.

Quick quiz

Answer these quick questions about Plot and structure:

1. Who was dead 'to begin with'?
2. Which relative comes to visit Scrooge, and for what reason?
3. Why does Scrooge refuse to give money to the charity collectors?
4. What weighs Marley down when he appears?
5. In Stave Two, where does the Spirit of Christmas Past first take Scrooge?

6. What has happened to Scrooge's sister, Fan, since she gave birth to Fred?
7. Why is Fezziwig throwing a party?
8. Why does Belle break off her engagement to Scrooge?
9. In Stave Three, what is the Ghost of Christmas Present surrounded by when it appears?
10. Where do poor families have their Christmas meal cooked?
11. How many rooms does Bob Cratchit's house have?
12. Who are Peter, Belinda and Martha?
13. Who are the two children at the feet of the Ghost?
14. In Stave Four, what colour is the Ghost of Christmas Yet to Come's hood?
15. Who is 'Old Scratch'?
16. How many people have stolen from Scrooge after he has died?
17. Who helps the family after the death of Tiny Tim?
18. What has changed about Scrooge's office?
19. In Stave Five, what can Scrooge hear outside when he wakes up?
20. Does Scrooge ever see any ghosts again after that Christmas Day?

Power paragraphs

Write **a paragraph in response to each of these questions**. For each, try to **use one quotation** you have learned from this section.

1. In what ways does Dickens contrast Fred and Scrooge in Stave One?
2. Why does Dickens choose to include the scene with Scrooge as a young schoolboy?

Exam practice

Reread the end of Stave Four where the Ghost of Christmas Yet to Come shows Scrooge his gravestone.

Why is this moment significant in the text as a whole? Write **two paragraphs** explaining your ideas. You could comment on:

- Scrooge's lack of understanding until this point
- the promise that he makes once he realises who is in the grave.

Five key things about Victorian life and society

1. **Queen Victoria** reigned from 1837 to 1901. *A Christmas Carol* was published in **1843**.

2. There was **rapid industrialisation** which meant growth in cities, creating opportunity but also overcrowding, poverty and hardship.

3. Hospitals were privately funded so ill people **had to pay** for their treatment. This meant poor people **suffered** the most.

4. **Schools were developing** in Victorian times but often children from poor families had to work instead of attending.

5. Dickens was one of the many **influential Victorians** who saw that social conditions were **unfair** and led to poverty and crime. He tried hard to change this.

What was Victorian London like?

- Victorian London was growing quickly in size and population.

- It had huge numbers of people living in poor conditions.

- Some parts of the city were very dangerous due to crime and poor sanitation.

- There were also areas of great wealth.

What was the Industrial Revolution?

- The Industrial Revolution began in the 18th century.

- This was a time when machines were invented to do the work of many people.

- Britain became a global centre of industry.

- Thousands of people flocked from the countryside to the cities to work in new factories.

- Factory workers were often poor, even though factories created huge wealth.

How were the poor treated?

- The Poor Law of 1834 sent unemployed people to harsh workhouses to discourage 'laziness'.
- Workhouses were huge prison-style buildings where families were separated.
- The poorest did piecework, such as making matches, or casual labour such as street sweeping.

Three key quotations

1. Commenting on the provision for the poor: 'The Treadmill and the Poor Law are in full vigour, then?' (Scrooge).
2. Describing part of London: 'The ways were foul and narrow ... the people half-naked, drunken, slip-shod, ugly.'
3. Poor living conditions: 'a wretched woman with an infant ... upon a door-step'.

Note it!

Athough Dickens was a rich and successful writer, he grew up in a family that suffered periods of poverty. Dickens had a horror of poverty and a firm belief in the importance of education. This explains why Dickens made the **'ragged'** child figures of Ignorance and Want so terrifying.

Exam focus

How do I link Victorian society to the novel? (AO3)

You can link to how Dickens presents support of the poor.

Dickens suggests that state support for the poor and uneducated is inadequate, and that personal kindness and commitment are needed. At the start of the novel, Scrooge asks the charity workers whether the 'Poor Law' is in operation, implying that's where his responsibility ends – even if workhouses are no better than prisons. It takes him until the end of the novel to understand that 'mankind' is his business, and he cannot turn his back on it.

- Topic sentence introducing key theme
- Gives historical context
- Links across novel
- Embedded quotation

Now you try!

Finish this paragraph about the presentation of the poor in the **novel**. Use one of the quotations from the list.

Conditions faced by the Victorian urban poor are explored by Dickens through the descriptions of London in the novel. For example, we see ....

SETTING AND CONTEXT Christmas and morality

Five key things about Christmas and morality

1. Many of our **ideas about Christmas** were popularised by Dickens and other Victorian writers.
2. Victorian Britain was **mainly Christian** and many people attended church.
3. Christmas was not as **widely celebrated** as today and many people worked on the day.
4. Many Victorians believed looking after the poor was a **moral duty**.
5. Some viewed poor people as 'immoral' if they turned to **crime**.

How did Dickens shape ideas about Christmas?

- Dickens popularised many of our Christmas traditions, such as the Christmas turkey.
- The Ghost of Christmas Present is surrounded by **'holly, mistletoe, and ivy'**.
- Dickens describes the idea of the Christmas spirit.
- Fezziwig's yard is an example of workplaces celebrating Christmas.
- Fred's family play **'wonderful games'** to celebrate the holiday.

What ideas about morality does Dickens present?

- Dickens believes that taking responsibility for each other is essential.
- Marley's punishment is to see others in need and not be able to help them.
- Scrooge's biggest fault is not caring about other people.
- The Cratchits demonstrate that family is more important than wealth.
- Fred shows that moral behaviour comes from kindness, not just giving money.

How important was Christianity in people's lives?

- In the mid nineteenth century, many people attended a church service regularly.
- However, the rise of scientific ideas meant many people questioned the Bible.
- Christianity was still the official religion of Britain.

Three key quotations

1. Fred's view of Christmas: 'a good time ... when men and women seem by one consent to open their shut-up hearts freely'.

2. Marley's Ghost's view of morality: 'charity, mercy, forbearance, and benevolence, were, all, my business'.

3. Christianity: workhouses 'scarcely furnish Christian cheer of mind or body to the multitude'.

Note it!

There are references to the Bible throughout the story. Tiny Tim says he hopes people will be reminded of Jesus, who made **'lame beggars walk'**, when they see his crutch, and Marley says he wishes that he had looked to the **'blessed star which led the Wise Men'** to the stable.

Exam focus

How can I write about Christmas and morality? AO3

You can use the **themes** of Christmas and morality to explore characters and events.

Dickens uses Marley's Ghost to explain to Scrooge the consequence of not living by Christian morals and putting money and business before people. Marley is literally weighed down by the chains that attach him to his money boxes and he is tortured by seeing poverty that he is now unable to help. Marley wishes he had made 'charity, mercy ... and benevolence' his 'business' and through this list Dickens conveys Marley's anguish and regret.

- Topic sentence
- Relevant detail
- Embedded quotation
- Identification of language feature

Now you try!

Finish this paragraph about the presentation of Christmas in the **novel**. Use one of the quotations from the list.

Dickens presents Fred as a character who embodies the spirit of Christmas when he explains to Scrooge the importance of ....

SETTING AND CONTEXT Settings

Five key things about settings in the novel

1. The **novel begins and ends in London**: in and around Scrooge's house and office.

2. Dickens was inspired by **real places** in London.

3. The Ghosts take us to **different settings** such as the miner's house and the lighthouse.

4. The **supernatural element** means the novel is set in the past, present and future.

5. We see some settings **change over time**, such as the decline in Scrooge's school.

How do Scrooge's house and office reflect his character?

- The office is cold and **'dismal'**, reflecting Scrooge's **'hard and sharp'** character.

- Scrooge's house is also dark and cold, with a **'low fire'**, conveying Scrooge's **'own low temperature'**.

What does Scrooge's school reveal about his childhood?

- Scrooge is a **'solitary'** child at the school, which foregrounds his adult life.

- The **'chilly bareness'** of the school suggests Scrooge's childhood was lonely and unhappy.

- The school is neglected and becomes **'darker and more dirty'** as Scrooge grows older.

In what ways are Christmas scenes important to the novel?

- London on Christmas Eve is a place **'full of glee'** that contrasts with Scrooge's feelings of resentment at missing a day's work, illustrated by his exclamation, **'Humbug'**. These scenes set out very clearly how Scrooge has cut himself off from the rest of society.

- In these scenes the Ghost shows Scrooge how Christmas is celebrated in even the harshest circumstances, such as on a ship at sea. Watching Fred's family play Christmas games makes even Scrooge feel **'gay and light of heart'**.

What do Old Joe's den and descriptions of the City reveal?

- Scrooge is taken to the financial heart of the city called the 'Change (short for Exchange), where he sees business people joking about him. Dickens reveals their unkindness and their unpleasant displays of wealth as they **'chink'** their money and show off their **'great gold seals'**.

- Old Joe's den is a place where thieves sell stolen goods. It's cramped and filthy, filled with **'unseemly rags'** and **'masses of corrupted fat'** (used to make soap, for example), reflecting the depths that poor people are forced to go to make money.

Quick quiz

Answer these quick questions about Settings and context:

1. Who were workhouses intended for?
2. Why did poor children often not go to school?
3. Why did the Industrial Revolution make people go to the cities?
4. Name an example of a workplace that celebrates Christmas in the story.
5. What was the main religion in Victorian Britain?
6. What was the temperature of Scrooge's office?
7. What could people do at Old Joe's den?
8. What does Scrooge say 'Humbug' to?
9. Who 'chinks' their money to show off their wealth?
10. Who wishes they had looked to the 'blessed star' that led the Wise Men to Jesus?

Power paragraphs

Choose one key setting or context related to the novel.

Write **two paragraphs** explaining how Dickens makes use of this setting or context in relation to either theme or character.

CHARACTERS Ebenezer Scrooge (Staves 1–3)

Five key things about Scrooge in Staves One to Three

1. Scrooge **hates** Christmas and feels **contempt** for the poor.
2. He is **visited by the Ghost** of his former business partner, Jacob Marley, to teach him a **lesson**.
3. He is made to **look back** on his childhood and early life.
4. He **remembers** how other people, such as Belle and Fezziwig, were important to him.
5. He is made to **confront** the poverty and misery all around him.

What do we learn about Scrooge in Staves One to Three?

- Scrooge works in the city in his cold and cramped office.
- His cold behaviour is reflected by his **'shrivelled'** and **'frosty'** appearance.
- He responds to the charity collectors' request for money with anger.
- Seeing his childhood is a **'softening influence'** on Scrooge.
- He was once engaged to Belle, but she ends the engagement as his love of money grows: **'You are changed.'**

How does Scrooge change in Staves One to Three?

- Scrooge is made to face up to the existence of ghosts and the afterlife.
- He learns that poverty and misery are all around him but he can do something to help.
- He learns how his past actions have led to his lonely life.
- The normally cold and detached Scrooge experiences strong emotions of fear, sympathy and regret, although he is not fully ready to change his ways yet.

Five key quotations

1. Scrooge's isolation: 'self-contained, and solitary as an oyster'.
2. His uncaring behaviour towards his employee Bob, suggesting it might be 'necessary for them to part'.
3. Scrooge on Christmas: 'every idiot who goes about with "Merry Christmas" on his lips, should be boiled with his own pudding'.
4. Scrooge caring too much about money: 'Another idol has displaced me' (Belle).
5. His developing emotions: 'he softened more and more'.

Note it!

Note that Scrooge has never **'painted out Old Marley's name'** from the sign above his warehouse. This suggests that Scrooge's life has not changed since Marley's death and that he cares so little that he has not even changed this sign.

Exam focus

How can I write about Scrooge at the start of the novel? AO1 AO2

You can comment on how Dickens presents Scrooge through his relationship with other characters.

> At the start of the story, Dickens presents Scrooge as being a bully to Bob Cratchit. When Bob tries to add coal to his fire, Scrooge threatens that it may be 'necessary for them to part' meaning he may sack Bob. Scrooge's detached language here implies his lack of empathy and that he does not take responsibility for his employee's suffering. Scrooge's changing attitude towards Bob will be a major part of his character development.

Topic sentence refers to specific point in novel

Relevant embedded quotation

Explains language effect

Link to rest of novel

Now you try!

Finish this paragraph about Scrooge's relationship with Belle.

Dickens explores Scrooge's changing character through his failed engagement to Belle. Belle ends their engagement because ....

Five key things about Scrooge in Staves 4 to 5

1. In Stave Four, Scrooge **no longer questions** the **Ghosts' message**.
2. He is shown the **contempt and fear** people have for him.
3. He is made to confront his **own death**.
4. He **completes his transformation** at the start of Stave Five.
5. He **learns the lesson** that **Jacob Marley** set out to teach him.

What do we learn about Scrooge in Staves Four to Five?

- Scrooge had no idea how badly he was regarded by business people in the City.
- He did not realise people hated him so much they would steal from his dead body.
- He is genuinely horrified at Tiny Tim's death, showing us his ability to have strong feelings.
- He laughs as he gets caught up in his stockings, showing he has a sense of humour.
- He can accept other people laughing at him but realises that **'nothing ever happened'** that did not make someone laugh.

How does Scrooge change?

- Scrooge becomes a good employer or **'master'**.
- He now enjoys being with people – he happily changes his mind and spends Christmas at Fred's.
- He makes a generous donation to the charity collection and apologises for his earlier unkindness.
- He becomes a full part of his family and of the Cratchits.

Five key quotations

1. Scrooge's new awareness: 'Avarice, hard dealing, gripping cares? They have brought him to a rich end, truly!'

2. His promise to the Ghost: 'The Spirits of all Three shall strive within me!'

3. His humour and fresh start in life: 'I don't know anything. I am quite a baby.'

4. His changed behaviour: 'to Tiny Tim, who did NOT die, he was a second father'.

5. He is happy and content: 'His own heart laughed: and that was quite enough for him.'

Note it!

Scrooge repeatedly refuses to look at the body of the dead man in Stave Four. Dickens builds suspense, delaying Scrooge's final moment of change, as he wonders who could be so hated that his death causes so little concern for those around him.

Exam focus

How can I write about Scrooge in Staves Three to Five?

You can comment on how Dickens presents Scrooge's reaction to seeing his own death.

In Stave Four, Dickens presents Scrooge as he watches people react to the death of 'someone' who was greedy and unkind. Scrooge learns important lessons from this and understands that 'avarice', or greed for wealth, has brought him to a 'rich' end. 'Rich end' here is a pun on the two meanings of the word 'rich', both as someone with money, but also as the Victorian slang word for 'terrible' or 'shocking'.

> Topic sentence refers to specific point in novel

> Relevant embedded quotation

> Language analysis

> Developed comment

Now you try!

Finish this paragraph about Scrooge in Staves Four and Five. Use one of the quotations from the list.

Dickens shows how Scrooge's behaviour becomes much kinder through the description of Scrooge's relationship with Tiny Tim, who ....

My progress Needs more work ☐ Getting there ☐ Sorted! ☐ 29

CHARACTERS Marley's Ghost and the Ghost of Christmas Past

Three key things about Marley's Ghost

1. Jacob Marley was Scrooge's **work partner**. He **died** seven years earlier and Scrooge has continue to run the business.

2. He first appears as a **face in Scrooge's doorknocker** and then again later in Scrooge's room following the ringing of the bells.

3. He is **punished for his greed** by dragging heavy chains and money boxes behind himself **for eternity**.

What is Marley's Ghost function in the novel?

- He starts off the supernatural aspect of the story by being the first ghost to appear to Scrooge.

- He explains that he now knows that caring for other people is more important than making money.

- He represents the horror of seeing other people in need and not being able to help.

Three key things about the Ghost of Christmas Past

1. The Ghost **shape-shifts**, looking both like an **old man** and a **young child**, and also a **candle-shaped light**.

2. It takes **Scrooge** back to his **childhood days** and shows Scrooge his **school**, his **first job** and his former sweetheart, **Belle**.

3. It **disappears** when Scrooge presses down the **'cap'** on its candle-like form and shuts off its light.

What is this Ghost's function in the novel?

- The Ghost wants Scrooge to understand how past events still have significance in the present.

- It introduces Scrooge's sister, Fan, Fezziwig and Belle, all of whom have disappeared from Scrooge's life and thoughts.

- It shines a light on Scrooge's background both literally and metaphorically.

Five key quotations

1. Marley's Ghost's chains: 'I wear the chain I forged in life.'

2. His punishment: 'No rest, no peace. Incessant torture of remorse.'

3. His lack of responsibility: 'Mankind was my business.'

4. The Ghost of Christmas Past: 'like a child: yet not so like a child as like an old man'.

5. Its light: 'would you so soon put out, with worldly hands, the light I give?'

Note it!

Dickens wanted to ensure that readers (and Scrooge) believed in the story's Ghosts. The opening line of the book is **'Marley was dead: to begin with'** and Dickens explains all the details around Marley's death, such as the burial and the will, to ensure this is seen as a fact!

Exam focus

How can I write about the Ghost of Christmas Past? AO1 AO2

You can comment on how Dickens uses language to describe the Ghost.

Dickens presents the Ghost as a paradoxical figure; 'like a child: yet not so like a child as an old man' – its hair is 'white, as if with age' but the skin shows the 'tenderest bloom'. The superlative adjective 'tenderest' suggests its skin is extremely soft, with connotations of youth. One of its functions is to prompt Scrooge to consider the lessons of youth and childhood and apply them in his older years.	Introductory topic sentence
	Embedded quotations
	Language detail
	Reference to key theme

Now you try!

Finish this paragraph about Marley's Ghost. Use one of the quotations from the list.

As Scrooge's deceased work partner, Marley's Ghost is used by Dickens to introduce Scrooge to the idea of being punished for . . . .

CHARACTERS The Ghosts of Christmas Present and Yet to Come

Three key things about the Ghost of Christmas Present

1. The Ghost of Christmas Present is **huge**, but fits supernaturally into any house or room.
2. It takes Scrooge to see various Christmas **celebrations**.
3. It also reveals the figures of **Ignorance** and **Want** hidden beneath its robes.

What is this Ghost's function in the novel?

- The Ghost of Christmas Present educates Scrooge about how Christmas may be celebrated, even in extreme poverty.
- It warns Scrooge that Tiny Tim may die if Scrooge does not learn its lessons.
- It reminds the reader of the 'Ignorance and Want' that lies beneath the surface of Victorian life.

Three key things about the Ghost of Christmas Yet to Come

1. This Ghost is **dressed in black** and does not reveal its face.
2. It **does not speak** to Scrooge and only points silently and significantly.
3. It **shows Scrooge** how people would react to his death and his **gravestone**.

What is the final Ghost's function in the novel?

- The Ghost of Christmas Yet to Come is a figure of Death that is more terrifying than all the other Ghosts.
- It shows Scrooge that his greedy life means no one would mourn his death.
- The sights and scenes that it shows Scrooge ensure that he will definitely change his ways.

Five key quotations

1. The Ghost of Christmas Present: 'there sat a jolly giant'.
2. Spreading Christmas spirit: 'How it ... opened its capacious palm ... with a generous hand, its bright and harmless mirth.'
3. The appearance of the Ghost of Christmas Yet to Come: 'a spectral hand and one great heap of black'.
4. Its firm purpose: 'The Spirit was immovable as ever.'
5. It shows pity for Scrooge at the graveside: 'The kind hand trembled.'

Note it!

The Ghost of Christmas Yet to Come is an **archetype** of Death in the style of the 'Grim Reaper'. But Stave Four has some dark humour, such as the arguing among the thieves and the City men's debate about whether **'lunch'** will be **'provided'** at Scrooge's funeral.

Exam focus

How can I write about the Ghost of Christmas Present?

You can comment on the context of Dickens's depiction of the Ghost of Christmas Present.

> Dickens celebrates the idea of the Victorian Christmas, with its huge feasts and great joy, and the 'jolly giant' of the Ghost of Christmas Present embodies those features. The Ghost is still frightening to Scrooge, who 'enters timidly' when it appears. Dickens believed in the 'spirit' of Christmas to do great good, but also reminds the reader that it cannot hide the 'Ignorance and Want' that exists just beneath the surface of Victorian society.

Introductory topic sentence

Embedded quotation

Knowledge about Dickens

Key theme of poverty

Now you try!

Finish this paragraph about the Ghost of Christmas Yet to Come. Use one of the quotations from the list.

The Ghost of Christmas Yet to Come does not speak to Scrooge, but it does respond when, at the end of Stage Four, Scrooge reacts with terror at the sight of ....

My progress Needs more work ☐ Getting there ☐ Sorted! ☐

Five key things about the Cratchits

1. The father, Bob Cratchit, is Scrooge's **poorly treated clerk** (a kind of secretary).

2. The Cratchits have **five children**. Peter and Martha are both young adults. The disabled Tiny Tim is the youngest child.

3. They live in an **overcrowded**, four-roomed house, sharing crockery and eating small meals, but are happy and loving.

4. Bob shows **no anger** towards Scrooge and wishes him well at Christmas.

5. The Cratchits are **central to Scrooge's transformation** into a kinder person.

What do we learn about the Cratchits at the beginning of the novel?

- Scrooge is so mean to Bob that he even claims Bob is **'picking'** his **'pocket'** by asking for a day off at Christmas.

- Bob Cratchit is so poor that he has no winter coat to wear and relies on a comforter (a scarf) to keep warm.

- Bob, despite his poverty and the cold, still runs home from work to play blindman's-buff, showing his child-like enjoyment of games.

- Mrs Cratchit does all she can to improve her household, such as making do by wearing cheap ribbons in her hair and dressing Peter in his father's best shirt.

- Even after the 'death' of Tiny Tim, Bob behaves kindly and gently **'and spoke pleasantly to all the family'**.

How do the Cratchits change?

- The Cratchits initially consider Scrooge as an **'Ogre'** but by the end of the **novel** welcome him to celebrate Christmas with them.

- Bob learns to enjoy having the new Scrooge as his employer. They allow Scrooge into their life as a **'second father'** to Tiny Tim.

- Tiny Tim does not recover from his disability, but is able to live comfortably with Scrooge's support.

Five key quotations

1. Bob's cold office: 'the clerk's fire was so very much smaller that it looked like one coal.'
2. Scrooge threatens Bob: 'you'll keep your Christmas by losing your situation'.
3. The loving Cratchit family: 'they were happy, grateful, pleased with one another'.
4. Bob is grateful for Scrooge's generosity: 'The Founder of the Feast!'
5. Tiny Tim's Christian message: 'God bless Us, Every One!'

Note it!

Dickens intended the character of Tiny Tim to be sympathetic. The word **'cripple'**, although not acceptable today, was in common use in Victorian times. Tiny Tim **symbolises** the **'surplus population'** that Scrooge says would be **'better'** to die. When Scrooge is faced with the reality of Tiny Tim's death he realises the cruelty of these words.

Exam focus

How can I write about the Cratchits? AO1 AO3

You can write about the Cratchits and the **theme** of family life.

> Dickens was keen to promote the importance of enjoying family life, having come from an unhappy and chaotic family. Despite their poverty, the Cratchits, alongside Fred's wealthier family and even Belle's family, are examples of people being 'grateful' for each other. Scrooge becomes a 'second father' to Tiny Tim, which is particularly significant considering Scrooge, like Dickens, appears to have had a distant relationship with his own father.

Introductory topic sentence

Links across the novel

Embedded quotation

Gives context of Dickens's own experiences

Now you try!

Finish this paragraph about Bob Cratchit. Use one of the quotations from the list.

The relationship between Scrooge and Bob conveys a great deal about their characters. Through the way Scrooge treats Bob at work, Dickens shows ....

My progress   Needs more work ☐   Getting there ☐   Sorted! ☐   **35**

CHARACTERS Fred and Fan

Three key things about Fred

1. Fred is **Scrooge's nephew**, the only son of Fan, Scrooge's sister.

2. He **appears three times** in the story: in Stave One when he visits Scrooge; Stave Three, when Scrooge observes the party at his house; and Stave Five when he welcomes Scrooge into his house.

3. He is mentioned by Bob in Stave Four as **showing kindness** to the Cratchits.

What is Fred's function in the novel?

- Fred acts as a **counterpoint** to Scrooge; where Scrooge is cold and icy, Fred is **'ruddy and handsome'** and has eyes that **'sparkled'**. Where he married for love, Scrooge separated from Belle, because she had no money.

- Through Fan he becomes a **symbol** of regret about family for Scrooge.

- He represents the Christian idea of forgiveness, leaving the invitation to Scrooge always open, despite his meanness.

Three key things about Fan

1. Fan is Scrooge's **sister**, younger than him, and Fred's mother. She has died before the **novel** begins.

2. She **appears once in the story** when she comes to **collect Scrooge from school**.

3. She is described as **'delicate'**, which may explain her **early death**.

What is Fan's function in the novel?

- Fan helps show that Scrooge had a difficult childhood with perhaps a violent father.

- She is another counterpoint to Scrooge with her kindness and tenderness towards him.

- She awakens a feeling of uneasiness in Scrooge about his behaviour towards Fred.

Five key quotations

1. 'Though it has never put a scrap of gold or silver in my pocket, I believe it has done me good' (Fred, about Christmas).

2. 'I mean to give him the same chance every year, whether he likes it or not, for I pity him' (Fred, about Scrooge).

3. '... he is the pleasantest-spoken gentleman you ever heard' (Bob about Fred).

4. 'Father is so much kinder than he used to be, that home's like heaven' (Fan about Scrooge's father).

5. 'Always a delicate creature .... But she had a large heart' (Ghost of Christmas Past about Fan).

Note it!

Note how Dickens explores the **theme** of how children are formed by their experiences through Fan's visit to Scrooge as a schoolboy. Elsewhere, Tiny Tim and the symbolic children 'Ignorance' and 'Want' also show the consequences of poverty, lack of education and general neglect.

Exam focus

How can I write about Fred's character?

You can comment on how Dickens uses Fred to communicate a message about Christmas.

One of Fred's functions is to represent a contrasting idea of the value of Christmas from that of Scrooge.	Topic sentence
He does not judge it in terms of its monetary value, saying that while it hasn't 'put a scrap of gold or silver' in his pocket, he feels better for the spirit of kindness it evokes.	Embedded quotation / Explains significance of quotation
This seems like a Christian message in Fred, as he appears to 'turn the other cheek' however unpleasantly his uncle behaves towards him.	Make link to theme of poverty

Now you try!

Finish this paragraph about Fan. Use one of the quotations from the list.

As Scrooge's little sister, Dickens uses Fan to show that Scrooge's childhood ......

CHARACTERS Mr Fezziwig and Belle

Three key things about Mr Fezziwig

1. Fezziwig was **Scrooge's first employer** when Scrooge was a young apprentice.

2. He is full of **fun and laughter** and his warehouse is **'snug, and warm, and dry'**.

3. The Ghost of Christmas Past shows Scrooge a **Christmas party** that Fezziwig held for all his staff at the warehouse where Scrooge worked with **'dances'**, **'a great piece of Cold Roast'** and **'plenty of beer'**.

What is Mr Fezziwig's function in the novel?

- Seeing Fezziwig reminds Scrooge of happier times in his life.

- Fezziwig takes responsibility for the happiness and welfare of his employees and so contrasts with Scrooge as an employer.

- He reminds Scrooge that people are more important than money, and **'the happiness he gives'** does not cost **'a fortune'**.

Three key things about Belle

1. Belle, a **'fair young girl'**, was Scrooge's fiancée when Scrooge was a young man.

2. Although she loves Scrooge and wants to marry him, she calls off their engagement because regretfully she can see that he loves **'the pursuit of wealth'** more than he loves her.

3. She goes on to marry someone else and has children and a happy home.

What is Belle's function in the novel?

- Seeing Belle reminds Scrooge that he missed a chance for happiness when he let their relationship end.

- Belle reveals to us that Scrooge's love of money has had an effect on him almost all his adult life.

- Belle's family home is **'full of comfort'** and serves as a contrast to Scrooge's lonely house.

Five key quotations

1. Fezziwig's generous manner: he 'laughed all over himself... and called out in a comfortable, oily, rich, fat, jovial voice'.

2. Fezziwig as an employer: 'he has the power to render us happy or unhappy' (Scrooge).

3. Scrooge's love of money: 'Another idol has displaced me' (Belle).

4. Scrooge's love of money has changed him: 'your nobler passions fall off one by one' (Belle).

5. 'I release you. With a full heart, for the love of him you once were.' (Belle, ending their engagement).

Note it!

Dickens uses an extended **metaphor** to convey how Scrooge's love of money as a young man changes him entirely. Dickens describes Scrooge's 'passion' for money taking 'root' in him. The growth overtakes him like the **'shadow of the growing tree'**. The **noun** 'shadow' implies the dark and terrible nature of Scrooge's greed.

Exam focus

How can I write about Fezziwig? AO1

You can comment on how Dickens presents Fezziwig as the model employer.

> Dickens presents Fezziwig as an example of how bosses could make a workplace a pleasant environment, at a time when there were few laws in place to protect workers. Fezziwig, unlike Scrooge, understands his 'power' and represents an example of how 'happy' workers, in a 'dry' and 'bright' workplace, will work hard for a company. Scrooge, in contrast, takes no responsibility for the wellbeing of his employee, Bob Cratchit.

- Introductory sentence, link to context
- Establishes connection between characters
- Embedded quotations
- Key theme

Now you try!

Finish this paragraph about Belle. Use one of the quotations from the list.

As Scrooge's former fiancée and only sweetheart, Belle is the first person to notice the effect that the love of money ....

My progress   Needs more work ☐   Getting there ☐   Sorted! ☐   **39**

CHARACTERS Quick revision

1. Look at this ideas map representing Scrooge. Can you find other quotes or details about Scrooge to add to the ideas map?

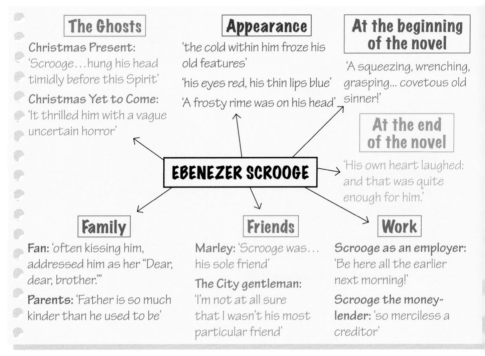

The Ghosts

Christmas Present: 'Scrooge…hung his head timidly before this Spirit'

Christmas Yet to Come: 'It thrilled him with a vague uncertain horror'

Appearance

'the cold within him froze his old features'

'his eyes red, his thin lips blue'

'A frosty rime was on his head'

At the beginning of the novel

'A squeezing, wrenching, grasping… covetous old sinner!'

At the end of the novel

'His own heart laughed: and that was quite enough for him.'

EBENEZER SCROOGE

Family

Fan: 'often kissing him, addressed him as her "Dear, dear, brother."'

Parents: 'Father is so much kinder than he used to be'

Friends

Marley: 'Scrooge was… his sole friend'

The City gentleman: 'I'm not at all sure that I wasn't his most particular friend'

Work

Scrooge as an employer: 'Be here all the earlier next morning!'

Scrooge the money-lender: 'so merciless a creditor'

2. Create your own ideas map for one of the other characters, or group of characters, such as the Ghosts or the Cratchit family.

Quick quiz

Answer these quick questions about Characters:

1. Who was Jacob Marley's only friend?
2. Who is the first character to visit Scrooge's office on Christmas Eve?
3. Who wears a white comforter instead of a winter coat?
4. Which object transforms into the face of Jacob Marley?
5. In Stave Two, whose childhood imaginary friends are 'Ali Baba' and 'Robinson Crusoe'?

6. With whom do Scrooge and Fan have a Christmas drink before le school?
7. Which Ghost has an 'extinguisher-cap' to put out its light?
8. What colour is the Ghost of Christmas Present's robe?
9. How many brothers does the Ghost of Christmas have?
10. How many shillings does Bob Cratchit earn a week?
11. What job does Martha Cratchit do?
12. Who does Bob Cratchit call the 'Founder of the Feast'?
13. Which Ghost takes Scrooge to a lighthouse and a ship?
14. At whose party do we meet a character called 'Topper'?
15. Whose nickname is 'Old Scratch'?
16. Who runs a shop that is filled with 'rags, bottles, bones, and greasy offal'?
17. What is Mrs Dilber's job?
18. Why are the young couple in Stave Four relieved to hear of Scrooge's death?
19. Who nearly cuts his nose off shaving in Stave Five?
20. How late is Bob to work on Boxing Day?

Power paragraphs

Write **a paragraph in response to these questions**. For each try to **use one quotation** you have learned from this section.

1. Explain the effect that the Ghost of Christmas Past has on Scrooge.
2. How does Dickens present the Cratchit family?

Exam practice

Reread the section in Stave Two when Scrooge watches Belle with her family at home, from 'And now Scrooge looked on more attentively than ever ...' to the end of the Stave.

What does Scrooge learn from watching Belle and her family at her house? Write **two paragraphs** explaining your ideas. You should comment on:

● how Dickens presents Belle and her family
● what kind of relationship Scrooge has with his own family.

Five key things about the theme of Christmas

1. Dickens's descriptions of Christmas have established many of our **modern ideas** of a traditional Christmas, such as the **Christmas dinner**.

2. The Ghost of Christmas Present is surrounded by the **traditional food and decorations** of Christmas such as holly, mistletoe and turkey.

3. The Ghost of Christmas Present **spreads the Christmas Spirit** everywhere it visits, even on board ships and below ground in mines.

4. **Christmas offers Scrooge all the opportunities** he needs to change, by joining in family events, donating money to charity and being kind to his employees.

5. Dickens reminds us of the **presence of the Church** at Christmas, with the **ringing of church bells** on Christmas day.

How is Christmas celebrated in the novel?

- The Cratchits celebrate Christmas by making the most of their meagre resources, such as their **'two tumblers, and a custard-cup without a handle'**.

- Fred's family celebrate Christmas through parties and games, such as **'blind-man's bluff'** and **'Yes and No'**.

- Scrooge experiences lonely childhood Christmases at school, **'a solitary child, neglected by his friends'**.

- Fezziwig shows the importance of a Christmas holiday from work, **'No more work tonight. Christmas Eve'**.

What does Dickens present as a traditional Christmas?

- Food: **'turkeys, geese, game, poultry, brawn'**.
- Decorations: **'The walls and ceiling were so hung with living green'**.
- Snow: **'the smooth white sheet of snow upon the roofs'**.
- People visiting each other: **'shadows on the window-blind of guests assembling'**.
- Christmas Blessings: **'God bless us every one!'**

Five key quotations

1. Scrooge links Christmas with financial loss: 'What's Christmas time to you but a time for paying bills without money' (Scrooge to Fred).
2. Scrooge dismisses Christmas: 'Bah! said Scrooge, 'Humbug!'
3. Christmas as a time for togetherness: 'men and women ... think of people below them as if they were really fellow-passengers to the grave' (Fred to Scrooge).
4. Poverty at Christmas: 'a time, of all others, when Want is keenly felt, and Abundance rejoices' (charity collectors).
5. Christmas brings Scrooge's greatest change: 'he knew how to keep Christmas well, if any man alive possessed the knowledge'.

Note it!

In Stave Five, Scrooge celebrates Christmas by pledging to donate a large amount of money. He says the collector is doing him a **'favour'**, that he is **'much obliged'** and that he thanks him **'fifty times'**. This **repetition** emphasises Scrooge's newfound generosity.

Exam focus

How can I write about the importance of Christmas? (AO1)

You can write about the ways Dickens presents Christmas.

Dickens presents the importance of Christmas across classes in Stave One when Fred uses the image of Christmas bringing people together as 'fellow-passengers', with people 'below them'. The phrase 'below them' implies that Christmas unites people from all different backgrounds. This links into Dickens's presentation of the Christmas spirit being shared in poor and remote locations, such as the Cratchits and the miners, as well as the wealthier families, such as Belle's and Fred's.

- Reference to specific detail
- A developed explanation
- Awareness of writer's intention
- Making links across text

Now you try!

Finish this paragraph about Christmas. Use one of the quotations from the list.

Dickens presents the images of Ignorance and Want to remind the reader that poverty ....

THEMES Responsibility

Five key things about the theme of responsibility

1. Dickens believed that we are all responsible for the **health and happiness** of the people around us.

2. Although there were **laws and charities** helping the poor in Victorian England, Dickens felt they did not do enough.

3. Marley's Ghost is the **first character** to explain to Scrooge the importance of taking responsibility for others with his statement, **'Mankind was my business.'**

4. The **Ghosts demonstrate** to Scrooge all the ways he is responsible for other people's welfare, beginning with the Cratchits.

5. Characters such as Fred and Fezziwig show that you can **increase your own happiness** when you take responsibility for other people.

When do people show responsibility in the novel?

- The charity collectors take some responsibility for the plight of the London poor and collect money to help them.

- Fan takes responsibility for her lonely brother's misery asking their father if Scrooge can come home from school.

- Fezziwig takes responsibility for his workers, ensuring their workplace is clean and bright and that they are happy and valued.

- The Cratchits take responsibility for each other's welfare.

- It's too late for ghosts like Marley to take responsibility for the less well-off and they are punished and **'inexpressibly sorrowful'** over this.

How does Scrooge show he takes responsibility for those around him?

- He donates a large sum of money to make up for his past meanness.

- He ensures the Cratchits have a happy Christmas by sending round a **'prize Turkey'**, even paying for a cab to carry it.

- He improves Bob Cratchit's working conditions.

- He becomes a good friend to all.

Five key quotations

1. Responsibility to others at Christmas: 'a kind, forgiving, charitable, pleasant time' (Fred).

2. Marley's Ghost's responsibilities: 'Mankind was my business. The common welfare was my business; charity, mercy, forbearance'.

3. Employers' responsibilities: 'He has the power ... to make our service light or burdensome; a pleasure or a toil' (Scrooge on Fezziwig).

4. Responsibility to improve: 'I will not shut out the lessons that they teach' (Scrooge).

5. Responsibility for others: 'I'll raise your salary, and endeavour to assist your struggling family' (Scrooge to Bob Cratchit).

Note it!

Scrooge argues that by paying taxes which fund the building of prisons and workhouses in their **'useful course'**, he is taking responsibility for the poor. Dickens repeatedly shows that this belief is incorrect, particularly when he introduces the child-like figures of 'Ignorance and Want'.

Exam focus

How does Dickens explore responsibility? (AO1)

You can write about Fred's positive attitudes to other people.

> Dickens explores the key idea of responsibility by contrasting Fred's attitudes to other people with Scrooge's. Fred loves Christmas partly because he sees it as a time when people are more 'charitable' towards each other, both in terms of gifts and donations as well as being 'kind' and 'forgiving'. This behaviour reflects his views on taking responsibility for each other's welfare and feelings. Scrooge, in contrast, sees Christmas as a time of financial loss.

- Overview of theme
- Embedded quotations
- Link to theme
- Comparison of characters

Now you try!

Finish this paragraph about responsibility. Use one of the quotations from the list.

Dickens shows that Scrooge has an opportunity for taking personal responsibility by helping the Cratchits ....

My progress Needs more work ☐ Getting there ☐ Sorted! ☐   45

Five key things about the theme of change and redemption

1. Redemption is closely linked to **Christian ideals** in which a person can be 'saved' from their evil ways.

2. Scrooge is **transformed** from a mean miser to a generous father figure.

3. He **redeems himself** via a series of actions to right the wrongs of the past.

4. The Ghosts enable Scrooge to **learn from the past** so that he can **change the future**.

5. Marley's Ghost is **punished forever** for **not changing** his own selfish ways.

What does redemption mean and why does Scrooge require it?

- Redemption means being saved from sin or wrong doing. Scrooge is described as a **'sinner'** at the start of the **novel**.

- Scrooge's main sin appears to be covetousness (being greedy for money), from which he needs redemption.

- Scrooge's greed is all the worse because the money he makes does not do any good. He does not even spend it on making himself comfortable.

- Belle says that Scrooge worships wealth as an **'idol'**. Scrooge needs to be redeemed because his love of money now prevents him from loving people.

What enables Scrooge to be redeemed – and how?

- Marley is the initial agent of change by showing Scrooge the punishment he suffers and saying that Scrooge is also **'captive, bound, and double-ironed'** by his love of money.

- Scrooge is redeemed by the Ghosts as they make him feel emotions he has forgotten, such as excitement for Christmas and sympathy for the poor.

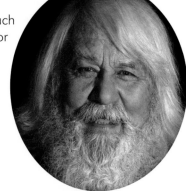

- Scrooge is redeemed through the Ghost of Christmas Yet to Come which terrifies Scrooge by showing him his lonely grave.

- Scrooge is ultimately redeemed by becoming a generous and loving man who shares his wealth.

Five key quotations

1. The Christmas Spirits bring change: 'Without their visits ... you cannot hope to shun the path I tread' (Marley's Ghost).
2. Scrooge's change: 'Your reclamation' (the Ghost of Christmas Past).
3. Tiny Tim, a motive for change: 'If these shadows remain unaltered by the Future, the child will die' (the Ghost of Christmas Yet to Come).
4. Scrooge's desire for redemption: 'I hope to live to be another man from what I was' (Scrooge to the Ghost of Christmas Yet to Come).
5. Scrooge transformed: 'Some people laughed to see the alteration in him'.

Note it!

Scrooge has a series of chances to change even in Stave One. Fred offers to reunite Scrooge with his family and Scrooge has an opportunity to donate money to the poor and even to be kinder to his employee. The transformed Scrooge takes all of these chances!

Exam focus

How does Dickens explore redemption? AO1 AO2

You can comment on how Dickens uses ideas of sin and redemption.

Dickens explores the key idea of redemption through Scrooge's journey, both literal and emotional, from a cruel and lonely man to a gentle father figure. When the Ghost of Christmas Past states it is there for Scrooge's 'reclamation', Dickens is referring to the idea of 'reclaiming' or bringing someone back from 'sin' to goodness. Biblical examples of sinners being redeemed, like Scrooge, would have been familiar to the Victorian reader.

- Topic sentence gives an overview of theme
- Relevant embedded quotation
- Fully explains meaning of word
- A link to context

Now you try!

Finish this paragraph about redemption. Use one of the quotations from the list.

Dickens shows that redemption is only possible when Scrooge fully understands the consequences ....

My progress Needs more work ☐ Getting there ☐ Sorted! ☐   47

Five key things about the theme of money and avarice

1. Avarice is greed for **wealth and money**.

2. Dickens treats avarice as a **sin**.

3. There were **great gaps** between the rich and the poor in Victorian society and Dickens tirelessly **campaigned to help the poor**.

4. Jacob Marley's Ghost is visibly **punished** for his avarice by having to drag his money boxes on chains for eternity.

5. Money and avarice **do not lead to happiness** in *A Christmas Carol*.

Where do we see money and avarice in the novel?

- We are told that Scrooge saved money when he organised Marley's funeral and **'solemnised it with an undoubted bargain'**.

- Scrooge's office is a **'counting-house'** and his business lends money, making a profit from interest charged on repayments.

- Belle is the first person to notice how avarice has changed Scrooge.

- The Ghost of Christmas Yet to Come shows Scrooge the couple who have been nearly **'ruined'** by the horror of being in debt to Scrooge, a **'merciless creditor'**.

How is money used for good?

- The charity collectors collect cash donations to help the poor.

- Scrooge notes it is impossible **'to add and count up'** Fezziwig's kindness, although he spends just **'three or four pounds'** on the Christmas party.

- The Cratchits use the little money they have to bring happiness to their family celebrations.

- Scrooge's first generous actions are to buy a turkey, pay for a cab (horse and carriage) and tip the boy, all of which he does with a **'chuckle'**.

Five key quotations

1. Scrooge saves money on lighting and heating: 'darkness is cheap, and Scrooge liked it'.
2. Marley's Ghost's chain **symbolises** his avarice: 'cash-boxes, keys, padlocks, ledgers, deeds, and heavy purses wrought in steel'.
3. Youthful Scrooge is changed by avarice: 'had begun to wear the signs of care and avarice'.
4. Victorian society claims to believe avarice is wrong: 'nothing it professes to condemn with such severity as the pursuit of wealth!' (Scrooge).
5. Scrooge on seeing his dead body: 'Avarice, hard dealing, griping cares? They have brought him to a rich end, truly.'

Note it!

Dickens is not suggesting that money is itself a bad thing. Scrooge does not give up his profession as a money-lender at the end of the novel. Dickens, instead, implies that what people do with their money can make a big difference and bring personal benefits, as it does for the transformed Scrooge.

Exam focus

How does Dickens explore money and avarice? AO1 AO2

You can write about how avarice controls Scrooge's behaviour.

Dickens explores the key idea of avarice through Scrooge's home. Scrooge lives in a building that he inherited from Marley and so cost him nothing. He also refuses to burn candles because 'darkness is cheap', eat anything more costly than 'gruel' or use more than a 'handful of fuel'. The details of the setting convey the way that Scrooge is obsessed with holding on to money for no good reason.

- Introduces key point
- Embedded quotations
- Linking key quotations
- Relevant technical language

Now you try!

Finish this paragraph about money and avarice. Use one of the quotations from the list.

Dickens presents Scrooge's final lesson about the effects of avarice when the Ghost of Christmas Yet to Come shows ....

Five key things about the theme of poverty and education

1. The Industrial Revolution encouraged **cities to expand** but this led to vast slums of poor people living in **terrible conditions**, like the area around Old Joe's shop.

2. The **Poor Law of 1834** was supposed to help **alleviate poverty**, but the workhouse system it created was cruel to the poor and unpopular.

3. Dickens **campaigned for education** to be offered to poor children as he believed this was a way out of poverty. Peter and Martha Cratchit, as children from a poor background and limited access to education, expect low-paid work.

4. Many of the poor people in the **novel** are in **work**, such as the Cratchits.

5. **Poverty and poor education are linked to crime**, e.g. Old Joe's behaviour.

Where is poverty depicted in *A Christmas Carol*?

- Bob Cratchit is unable to afford a winter coat and Mrs Cratchit dresses **'but poorly in a twice-turned gown'**.
- The charity collectors are raising money for the **'poor and destitute'**.
- The childlike figure of **'Want'**.
- Scrooge is taken to an **'obscure'** part of London with **'straggling'** streets full of the poor.

How is education presented in *A Christmas Carol*?

- Scrooge's school is represented as lonely and unfriendly: **'a long, bare, melancholy room'**.
- Scrooge's headteacher is described as treating him with **'ferocious condescension'** suggesting a lack of personal concern.
- Fan does not attend school – it was common for families not to send all their children to school and girls were often taught at home.
- The childlike figure of **'Ignorance'** represents the lack of basic education offered to most children.

Five key quotations

1. At first Scrooge connects money with happiness: 'What reason have you to be merry? You're poor enough.'

2. Christmas should not be linked to poverty or wealth: 'though it has never put a scrap of gold or silver fold in my pocket, I believe that it has done me good' (Fred).

3. Victorian poverty: 'hundreds of thousands are in want of common comforts' (the charity collectors).

4. Ignorance and want are **symbols** of poverty and lack of education: 'no perversion of humanity ... has monsters half so horrible and dread'.

5. Lack of education is worse than poverty: 'most of all beware this boy, for on his brow I see written that which is Doom' (the Ghost of Christmas Present).

Note it!

In *A Christmas Carol* the figure of 'Ignorance', who symbolises lack of education, is described as **'Doom'** – a greater threat than poverty in itself. To the Victorian reader 'doom' would suggest real catastrophe or ruin.

Exam focus

How does Dickens present poverty and education? AO1

You can write about the link between Christmas and poverty.

Dickens highlights the idea of poverty by setting the novel over Christmas, a time that can make poverty even harder to bear. Although Scrooge and Fred are not in poverty, Scrooge still judges Christmas through its financial implications, suggesting that if you are 'poor' you cannot be 'merry' but Fred, Fezziwig and the Cratchits all demonstrate you can be happy without a great deal of money.

- Introduction to theme
- Embedded quotations
- Connecting characters together
- Explaining a key theme

Now you try!

Finish this paragraph about poverty and education. Use one of the quotations from the list.

Dickens conveys the plight of the poor when the charity collectors ....

Five key things about the theme of family

1 Dickens had a **difficult family life**, but believed in the importance of families, and presents family as a key factor in Scrooge's redemption.

2 Scrooge's lonely childhood and school days reflect a **limited family life**.

3 Seeing Belle's loving family life makes Scrooge reflect on the **benefits** family can bring.

4 Family life can **support** people **even in great hardship**, such as the Cratchits.

5 It was normal in Victorian times to have many children, but Scrooge is **distanced from his father** and neither he nor Marley have children.

What do examples of family life teach Scrooge?

- The happy families, such as Belle's, show Scrooge the joy of sharing his life with others and contrast with his own isolation.

- Colleagues can be like family and Fezziwig's family welcomes in the workers on Christmas Eve.

- Fred's family is loving and caring and welcomes Scrooge, showing forgiveness and compassion.

- The Cratchits are a struggling family but their simple enjoyment of games and conversation sustains them.

How does family help to change Scrooge?

- Watching Fezziwig and his family prompts Scrooge to be kinder to Bob.

- Fred always makes sure Scrooge knows he is welcome to join them.

- Seeing his sister, Fan, reminds Scrooge of how much she loved and supported him.

- The Cratchits are a family that benefit greatly from Scrooge's kindness.

Five key quotations

1. Scrooge welcomed by his family. 'Don't be angry, uncle. Come! Dine with us tomorrow!' (Fred).

2. Scrooge's family in the past: 'Father is so much kinder than he used to be, that home's like Heaven!' (Fan).

3. Belle's loving family: 'The joy, and gratitude, and ecstasy!'

4. The close family of Cratchits: 'they were happy, grateful, pleased with one another, and contented with the time'.

5. Scrooge rejoins his family: 'He was at home in five minutes. Nothing could be heartier.'

Note it!

Dickens does not introduce the reader to Scrooge's parents. Scrooge is sent away for long stretches to boarding school, even over Christmas, and it is not until he is **'a man'** that he is allowed to leave school and come home, following Fan's appeal to their father.

Exam focus

How do I write about family?

You can write about family through the presentation of Belle.

Dickens's presentation of Belle's family reminds Scrooge that he missed the chance to marry the woman he loved and the chance to have a family with a daughter to be his 'spring-time in the haggard winter of his life'. Dickens uses humorous hyperbole at the family's 'joy, gratitude, and ecstasy' that the baby has not swallowed a toy turkey, but Scrooge leaves the scene with tears in his eyes.

- Relevant detail relating to theme
- Embedded quotation
- Language feature noted
- Recognition of change in tone

Now you try!

Finish this paragraph about family. Use one of the quotations from the list.

Dickens regularly reminds the reader that Scrooge actually has a loving family. The first visitor to his office is ....

My progress Needs more work ☐ Getting there ☐ Sorted! ☐ 53

1. Look at this ideas map representing Christmas. Is there anything you could add?

The Ghosts

- The Three Spirits are all linked to Christmas:
- **Christmas Past:** shows Scrooge his lonely Christmas at school
- **Christmas Present:** 'taught Scrooge his precepts' and Scrooge how to celebrate Christmas through spreading the Christmas 'Spirit'

The Joy of Christmas

- 'it is good to be children sometimes, and never better than at Christmas'
- 'a flushed and boisterous group, just in time to greet the father...laden with Christmas toys and presents'

Scrooge hates Christmas

'Out upon Merry Christmas! What good had it ever done to him?'

Christmas in lonely and dangerous places

- On the lighthouse: 'they wished each other Merry Christmas in their can of grog'
- On the boat at sea: 'every man on board... had a kinder word for another that day'

CHRISTMAS

A traditional Christmas

- 'there was an air of cheerfulness'
- 'everything was good to eat and in its Christmas dress'
- 'the pudding, like a speckled cannon-ball'

Ignorance and Want

Ignorance and Want live beneath the robes of the Ghost of Christmas Present: 'They are Man's... they cling to me, appealing from their fathers'

2. Create your own ideas map for one of the other **themes**, such as responsibility or money and avarice.

Quick quiz

Answer these quick questions about Themes:

1. Which family has only three pieces of glassware in the house?
2. Which family plays music and sings songs on Christmas day?
3. How does the Scrooge send the turkey to the Cratchits?
4. What is the first thing Scrooge hears on Christmas Day?
5. Who says 'Mankind was my business'?
6. Who wails because they can no longer help people in need?

7. Who takes responsibility for Scrooge's misery at school?
8. Which Ghost says it has come for Scrooge's 'reclamation'?
9. What practical change does Scrooge make to the office to improve conditions?
10. What will happen to Tiny Tim if Scrooge does not change?
11. What happens when Scrooge tries to put on his stockings on Christmas morning?
12. How does the Ghost of Christmas Present change through the night?
13. Scrooge's greed makes him 'as sharp as flint'. What is 'flint'?
14. How many days a year does Bob Cratchit have off work?
15. Who works in 'a sort of tank' because of Scrooge's meanness?
16. Which poor character might have known 'the inside of a pawnbroker's'.
17. Why does Dickens think 'Ignorance' is worse than 'Want'?
18. Whose name is the answer to Fred's family guessing game?
19. Which members of the Cratchit family go out to work?
20. How many children did Fan have before she died?

Power paragraphs

Write **a paragraph in response to these questions**. For each, try to **use one quotation** you have learned from this section.

1. Explain how the visit from Jacob Marley's Ghost explores the theme of responsibility.
2. What does the character of Fred convey about the theme of family?

Exam practice

Reread the section in Stave One when Dickens describes Scrooge at home, from 'Up Scrooge went, not caring a button for that' to 'Humbug! said Scrooge; and walked across the room'. How does Dickens suggest his avarice and fear of spending money here and elsewhere in the book?

Write **two paragraphs** explaining your ideas. You should comment on:

- how Dickens presents Scrooge's home
- how Scrooge's avarice is also reflected in his office.

LANGUAGE Imagery and vocabulary

Five key things about Dickens's use of imagery and vocabulary

1 Dickens uses powerful **imagery**, e.g. the money-boxes attached to Marley's Ghost that **symbolise** his greed.

2 He uses **simile** and **metaphor** to help the reader understand character and relationships.

3 He **personifies** settings, e.g. the streets of London, and sometimes **themes**, to make them memorable.

4 He uses detailed **vocabulary** to depict people, settings, ideas and so on.

5 He uses **onomatopoeic** names (or **characternyms**) to convey information about characters, e.g. **'Scrooge'** sounds like 'scrounge' and 'squeeze'.

How does Dickens use imagery and themes?

- Dickens uses symbolism, e.g. Ignorance and Want are presented as two childlike figures who emerge from beneath the Spirit's cloak – their **'claws'** and **'wolfish'** appearance present a frightening idea of poverty.

- He suggests the spirit of Christmas in the image of the **'solitary lighthouse'**, set in a bleak landscape, where the keepers gather around a fire to sing a **'sturdy song'**.

How does Dickens use simile and metaphor to construct character?

- Dickens describes facial features and gestures, e.g. in Scrooge's **'frosty rime'** on his head, and the **'cold within him'** which freezes his features.

- He shows the contrasting side of humanity in characters such as Fezziwig whose legs shine **'like moons'** during the Christmas dance in the office.

How does Dickens use detailed vocabulary to create impact?

- Dickens uses lists of related nouns or **noun phrases** to suggest ideas, e.g. the Ghost of Christmas Present's rich throne of **'red-hot chestnuts, cherry-cheeked apples, juicy oranges'** conveys plenty and celebration.

- He often describes the smallest details to bring a place to life, such as the **'squeak and scuffle'** of mice and the **'half-thawed water-spout'** of Scrooge's school.

Five key quotations

1. **Simile:** describing character, 'I am as light as a feather!' (Scrooge).
2. **Personification:** describing place, the graveyard is 'fat with repleted appetite'.
3. **Symbolism:** in the Ghost of Christmas Past demonstrating different stages in life, hair that is 'white as if with age' but skin with 'tenderest bloom'.
4. **Lists:** Scrooge's list foods that can cause hallucinations to argue that Marley's Ghost is not real, 'undigested bit of beef, a blot of mustard, a crumb of cheese'.
5. **Characternym:** Fezziwig 'fizzes' with fun – 'wig' sounds like 'jig' or 'gig' suggesting movement.

Note it!

The word **'Humbug!'** is used by Scrooge to express his feelings about Christmas. A 'humbug' was something that was untrue or fraudulent and although Dickens did not make it up, it is now always associated with *A Christmas Carol*.

Exam focus

How can I write about Dickens's use of imagery? AO2

You can write about the imagery of plenty at Christmas.

Dickens develops the theme of avarice through imagery. The Spirit of Christmas Present's throne of 'turkeys, geese, game, poultry' and other festive foods shows what is available to the lucky few. The nouns are piled up like the throne itself – to the extent it is almost too much. Dickens wants Scrooge and the reader to make the contrast with the Cratchits who have so little in comparison.

Topic sentence about the theme	
Evidence for first statement	
Analysis of language technique	
Summative point linking to other characters	

Now you try!

Finish this paragraph about the use of simile. Use one of the quotations from the list.

Scrooge's description of himself at the end of the novel shows how much he has changed. He uses a simile to say he is ....

LANGUAGE Narrative style and voice

Five key things about Dickens's use of narrative style and voice

1. Dickens uses a narrative **voice** that tells an **engaging story**.

2. The narrative voice sometimes makes **political comments**, such as reflecting on the treatment of the poor.

3. The story is mostly written in the **third person** but sometimes uses a **first-person narrative** voice.

4. Using **long and short sentences** conveys complex and lively descriptions of places and people.

5. The narrative style includes frequent use of **dialogue**, **expressing the characters' personalitie**s through their own words.

How does Dickens use the first person to create the narrative voice?

- Dickens asks **'any man explain to me'** how Scrooge can see Marley's face in the doorknocker. This creates a sense that the **narrator** is just explaining what happened, as if it was true.

- The narrative voice sometimes reflects Dickens's own personality, e.g. when observing Belle's family: **'What would I not have given to be one of them!'**

How does Dickens use narrative voice to make social comments?

- The narrative voice addresses Death directly, **'Oh cold, cold, rigid, dreadful Death, set up thine altar here'**, to convey its ultimate power.

- The narrative voice explains some characters' situations, e.g. Dickens comments on Bob Cratchit's poverty: **'Think of that! Bob had but fifteen "Bob" a-week himself'**.

How does Dickens use dialogue to create character?

- Dickens uses distinctive **vocabulary** in a character's dialogue, e.g. Fezziwig's **phrases 'Yo ho, my boys!'** and **'Hilli-ho!'** suggest his great energy.

- Dickens conveys Old Joe's working-class status through his accent, e.g. he says **'an't'** (isn't) and **''em'** (them).

Five key quotations

1. An engaging narrative voice: 'who knew his business better than you or I could have told it to him!' (on Fezziwig's violinist).

2. Social comment: 'it was a shame to quarrel on Christmas day. And so it was! God love it, so it was!'

3. First-person voice: 'as close to it as I am now to you' (about the Ghost of Christmas Past at Scrooge's bedside).

4. Long sentences: 'He was conscious of a thousand odours floating in the air, each one connected with a thousand thoughts, and hopes, and joys, and cares' (carrying Scrooge back in time).

5. Scrooge's unfriendly tone, declaring 'Good afternoon' five times.

Note it!

Dickens moves between first- and third-person voice, because this story is designed for reading aloud. Sentences such as **'The curtains of his bed were drawn aside, I tell you, by a hand'** sound as if the storyteller is watching the events as they happen.

Exam focus

How can I write about Dickens's use of narrative voice? AO2

You can write about how Dickens uses the first-person voice to convey character.

> Dickens describes Fezziwig's violinist informally as 'an artful dog, mind!' and as a man who 'knew his business better than you or I' which uses the first-person voice 'you or I', creating a close connection between the narrator and the reader. This is humorous but also makes serious social comment.

Language term

Embedded, connected quotations

Describing effect of language use

An overall point about the subject

Now you try!

Finish this paragraph about the use of dialogue. Use one of the quotations from the list.

Scrooge's way of talking throughout the novel reflects his gradual change in personality. In Stave One his dialogue conveys his ....

LANGUAGE Mood and atmosphere

Five key things about Dickens's use of mood and atmosphere

1. The **mood** of the **novel** can change from humour to fear, fun to seriousness.
2. Dickens describes the Christmas atmosphere through detail and **imagery**.
3. Dickens uses **pathetic fallacy** to reflect Scrooge's mood.
4. Each **setting** in the story has a different mood and atmosphere.
5. Dickens creates mood and atmosphere through use of **adjectives**.

How does Dickens create different moods and atmospheres?

- Dickens creates humour through exaggeration, **irony** and contrast, e.g. in the way Bob Cratchit **'involuntarily applauded'** Fred's praise for Christmas. The humour is created by the contrast between Scrooge's and Bob's attitudes towards Christmas.
- The Ghosts create a mood of fear through presentation of the unknown and powerful, especially the **Gothic** imagery of the Ghost of Christmas Yet to Come, whose **'ghostly eyes'** are hidden by its black garment.

How does Dickens create a Christmas atmosphere?

- Dickens uses lists to convey an atmosphere of plenty: **'sucking pigs, long wreaths of sausages, mince-pies, plum-puddings'**.

- He portrays London in the snow, using the whiteness to create beauty, **'the smooth white sheet'**, and fun, with the Londoners **'exchanging a facetious snowball'**.

How does Dickens use pathetic fallacy to convey Scrooge's mood?

- At the beginning of the novel Scrooge is described as **'frosty'** and the weather in Stave One is **'cold, bleak, biting'** with fog so dense that **'the houses opposite were mere phantoms'**. These details mirror Scrooge's cold and blind approach to life.
- In Stave Five, Scrooge is **'light'** and **'merry'** as reflected in the weather, **'No fog, no mist … Golden sunlight'**.

How does each setting have a different atmosphere?

- The Cratchits' house is small but it has an atmosphere of love and togetherness and the **'bustle'** of family life, with each family member taking on domestic jobs such as **'the plates being changed by Miss Belinda'** as they are unable to afford servants or a cook.
- Scrooge's office has an atmosphere of misery and meanness, which reflects his personality, with Bob Cratchit's **'dismal little cell'** implying the office is more like a prison than a place of work.

Quick quiz

Answer these quick questions about Language:

1. Which terrifying characters are described with the adjective 'wolfish'?
2. What language technique is Dickens using when he describes apples as 'cherry-cheeked'?
3. What did the **slang** word 'humbug' actually mean?
4. What effect does the list 'cash-boxes, keys, padlocks, ledgers, deeds' have when describing Marley's chain?
5. Identify the adjectives in this description: 'Tiny Tim was growing strong and hearty.'
6. What does the nickname 'Old Scratch' convey about Scrooge?
7. Which character's **dialogue** contains the **phrase** 'Yo ho, my boys!'?
8. In which person are the pronouns 'I' and 'me'?
9. 'The Grocers'! oh the Grocers'!' What mood is Dickens creating with this description of Christmas?
10. Dickens says Mrs Dilbert 'slunk' into Old Joe's shop. What mood does the **verb** 'slunk' convey?

Power paragraphs

Choose one key character other than Scrooge in the novel.

Write **two paragraphs** explaining how Dickens makes use of different language techniques to bring the character to life.

Five key things about the exam

1. You will have **one** question on *A Christmas Carol* which will be based on a **passage** given to you on the exam paper.

2. It will focus on **Dickens's presentation** of an aspect of the **novel**, such as a **character**, **relationship** or a **theme**.

3. You will have about **45–50 minutes** to read and respond to the question.

4. The question is worth **30 marks**.

5. The question assesses **AOs 1, 2 and 3**. Remember that **AO3** relates to 'context'.

What will a question look like?

> 1. Starting with this extract, explore how Dickens presents Scrooge's transformation at the end of the novel.
>
> Write about:
>
> - how Dickens presents Scrooge as someone who has been transformed in this extract
> - how Dickens presents Scrooge's transformation in the novel as a whole.
>
> [30 marks]

You must refer to the given passage

You must explain the techniques Dickens uses

This is the area you must tackle

A reminder to begin with the given extract

A reminder to **also** write about the whole of the novel

Do all questions look the same?

- Not all questions will begin this way. Some might contain statements you debate. For example, **'Dickens's presentation of Scrooge enables the reader to feel sympathy for him.' Starting with this extract, explore how far you agree with this opinion.**

- Not all questions will be about a single character. Some might ask you about a relationship between two characters, e.g. between Scrooge and Fred.

What do I need to do to get a good mark?

Use this grid to understand your current level and how to improve it:

	AO1 Read, understand, respond	**AO2** Analyse language, form, structure and effects	**AO3** Show understanding of contexts
High	• You make **precise references** to the **passage** and *A Christmas Carol* **as a whole**. • Your argument is **well-structured**, with quotations **fluently embedded** in sentences. • You cover **both** the extract and the whole novel.	• You **analyse** and **interpret** the methods Dickens uses **very effectively**. • You **explore thoughtfully** the effects of these on the reader. • You show **excellent use** of subject terminology.	• You make **detailed, relevant links** between specific elements of the novel and social and/ or historical contexts.
Mid	• You make a **range of references** to the passage and the novel as a whole. • You respond in **a clear, logical way** with **relevant** quotations chosen.	• You **explain clearly** some of the methods Dickens uses, and **some effects** on the reader. • You use **mostly relevant** subject terminology.	• You show **clear evidence** of understanding context which is linked to the novel in places.
Lower	• You make **some references** to the passage and novel as a whole, but in rather a **patchy** way. • You make **some useful points** but evidence is **not always clear or relevant**.	• You make **occasional attempts** to explain Dickens's methods but a little **unclear**. • You show **some use** of subject terminology.	• You demonstrate **basic awareness** of context but **links** to the novel are **undeveloped** and **not always relevant**.

EXAM PRACTICE Character questions

Read this exam-style character question

Read this extract from Stave One in which Fred, has come to wish Scrooge a Merry Christmas. Then answer the question that follows.

> 'Nephew!' returned the uncle, sternly, 'keep Christmas in your own way, and let me keep it in mine.'
> 'Keep it!' repeated Scrooge's nephew. 'But you don't keep it.'
> 'Let me leave it alone, then,' said Scrooge. 'Much good may it do you! Much
> 5 good it has ever done you!'
> 'There are many things from which I might have derived good, by which I have not profited, I dare say,' returned the nephew: 'Christmas among the rest. But I am sure I have always thought of Christmas time, when it has come round – apart from the veneration due to its sacred name and origin, if anything
> 10 belonging to it can be apart from that – as a good time: a kind, forgiving, charitable, pleasant time: the only time I know of, in the long calendar of the year, when men and women seem by one consent to open their shut-up hearts freely, and to think of people below them as if they really were fellow-passengers to the grave, and not another race of creatures bound on other
> 15 journeys. And therefore, uncle, though it has never put a scrap of gold or silver in my pocket, I believe that it *has* done me good, and *will* do me good; and I say, God bless it!'
> The clerk in the tank involuntarily applauded: becoming immediately sensible of the impropriety, he poked the fire, and extinguished the last frail
> 20 spark for ever.
> 'Let me hear another sound from *you*' said Scrooge, 'and you'll keep your Christmas by losing your situation. You're quite a powerful speaker, sir,' he added, turning to his nephew. 'I wonder you don't go into Parliament.'
> 'Don't be angry, uncle. Come! Dine with us to-morrow.'

2. Starting with this extract, explore how Dickens presents Fred's attitudes towards other people.

Write about:

- how Dickens presents Fred's attitudes towards other people in this extract
- how Dickens presents Fred's attitudes towards other people in the novel as a whole.

[30 marks]

NOW read this further character question

Read this extract from Stave Three in which Scrooge meets the Ghost of Christmas Present. Then answer the question that follows.

Scrooge entered timidly, and hung his head before this Spirit. He was not the dogged Scrooge he had been; and though the Spirit's eyes were clear and kind, he did not like to meet them.

'I am the Ghost of Christmas Present,' said the Spirit. 'Look upon me!'

5 Scrooge reverently did so. It was clothed in one simple deep green robe, or mantle, bordered with white fur. This garment hung so loosely on the figure, that its capacious breast was bare, as if disdaining to be warded or concealed by any artifice. Its feet, observable beneath the ample folds of the garment, were also bare; and on its head it wore no other covering than a holly wreath,

10 set here and there with shining icicles. Its dark brown curls were long and free: free as its genial face, its sparkling eye, its open hand, its cheery voice, its unconstrained demeanour, and its joyful air. Girded round its middle was an antique scabbard; but no sword was in it, and the ancient sheath was eaten up with rust.

15 'You have never seen the like of me before!' exclaimed the Spirit.

'Never,' Scrooge made answer to it.

'Have never walked forth with the younger members of my family; meaning (for I am very young) my elder brothers born in these later years?' pursued the Phantom.

20 'I don't think I have,' said Scrooge. 'I am afraid I have not. Have you had many brothers, Spirit?'

'More than eighteen hundred,' said the Ghost.

'A tremendous family to provide for!' muttered Scrooge.

The Ghost of Christmas Present rose.

'Spirit,' said Scrooge submissively, 'conduct me where you will. I went forth last night on compulsion, and I learnt a lesson which is working now. To-night, if you have aught to teach me, let me profit by it.'

3. 'Dickens presents the three Christmas Ghosts as powerful characters.' Starting with this extract, explore how far you agree with this opinion.

Write about:

● how Dickens presents the Christmas Ghost as a powerful character in this extract

● how Dickens presents the three Christmas Ghosts as powerful characters in the novel as a whole.

[30 marks]

Five key stages to follow

1. **Read** the **question**; **highlight** key words.
2. **Read** the **passage** with the **key words** from the **question** in mind.
3. Quickly **generate ideas** for your response.
4. **Plan** for paragraphs.
5. **Write** your response; **check it** against your plan as you progress.

What do I focus on?

Highlight the **key words**:

2. Starting with this extract, explore how Dickens presents Fred's attitudes towards other people.

   Write about:

   - how Dickens presents Fred's attitudes towards other people in this extract
   - how Dickens presents Fred's attitudes towards other people in the novel as a whole.

What do they tell you? Focus on both extract and the whole text; explain what specific methods Dickens uses; stick to Fred's attitudes as the main topic.

How should I read the passage?

- Check for any immediate links to the question (e.g. Fred's discussion of other people's behaviour at Christmas; his relationship with Scrooge).
- Look for any evidence or quotations you could highlight (e.g. **'fellow-passengers to the grave'**).

How do I get my ideas?

Note your ideas in a spider diagram or list them in a table:

The extract	Fred's attitudes towards other people	The novel as a whole
Kind towards Scrooge: 'Come! Dine with us to-morrow.'		*Supports the Cratchit family when Tiny Tim dies: Mrs Cratchit says 'he's a good soul'.*
Does not want Scrooge to be angry: 'I ask nothing of you; why cannot we be friends?'		*Is shown to have a happy marriage: 'Scrooge's niece, by marriage, laughed as heartily as he.'*

The extract	The novel as a whole
• Kind towards Scrooge: 'Come! Dine with us to-morrow.' • Does not want Scrooge to be angry/lonely: 'I ask nothing of you; why cannot we be friends?'	• Supports the Cratchit family when Tiny Tim dies: Mrs Cratchit says 'he's a good soul'. • Has a happy marriage: 'Scrooge's niece, by marriage, laughed as heartily as he.'

HOW do I structure my ideas?

Make a **plan** for **paragraphs**.* Decide the order for your points:

- Paragraph 1: Go straight into your first point: *Fred, in contrast to Scrooge, feels kindly to other people.*
- Paragraph 2: *Fred's annual Christmas invitation to Scrooge.*
- Paragraph 3: *Fred's description of Christmas reflects his attitude towards other people.*
- Paragraph 4: *Fred's connection to Bob Cratchit, helping later in the story.*
- Paragraph 5: *Fred's character links to themes of family and responsibility.*

HOW do I write effectively?

Write **clear**, **analytical** paragraphs and **embed** evidence fluently. For example:

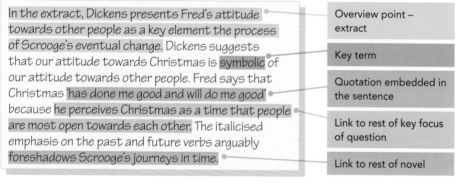

In the extract, Dickens presents Fred's attitude towards other people as a key element the process of Scrooge's eventual change. Dickens suggests that our attitude towards Christmas is symbolic of our attitude towards other people. Fred says that Christmas 'has done me good and will do me good' because he perceives Christmas as a time that people are most open towards each other. The italicised emphasis on the past and future verbs arguably foreshadows Scrooge's journeys in time.

Overview point – extract

Key term

Quotation embedded in the sentence

Link to rest of key focus of question

Link to rest of novel

Now you try!

Re-read Question 3 on page 65 and plan your response in the same way.

---

* The plan above and the sample answers on pages 68 and 70 have five paragraphs, but you don't need to be limited to this if you have more points to include (and time to write them!).

What does a Grade 5 answer look like?

Read the task again, then the sample answer below.

2. Starting with this extract, explore how Dickens presents Fred's attitudes towards other people.

Write about:

- how Dickens presents Fred's attitudes towards other people in this extract
- how Dickens presents Fred's attitudes towards other people in the novel as a whole. **[30 marks]**

In the passage, Fred shows a kind and thoughtful attitude towards other people. Dickens shows this by the way Fred visits Scrooge to invite him to Christmas dinner even though Scrooge tells him 'keep Christmas in your own way and let me keep it in mine'. The phrase 'in your own way' implies that Scrooge does not have the same attitude to Fred and this shows the contrast between them.

Fred's attitude towards other people is also shown through the way that he talks about Christmas. He believes that relationships with each other are more important than making money. Fred says he has 'not profited' from Christmas in terms of 'gold or silver', but Christmas is important because it is a time 'when men and women seem by one consent to open their shut-up hearts freely' which means being more open and friendly towards each other. Fred's thoughtful attitude towards other people is also influenced by Christmas's religious message, which he refers to explicitly when he mentions 'the veneration due to its sacred name and origin'.

The word 'shut-up' links to Dickens's descriptions of Scrooge as 'self-contained' in an earlier Stave, developing the contrast between the two characters' attitudes towards other people. Bob Cratchit 'applauded' in agreement with Fred. Fred has a friendly attitude towards other people. He doesn't even get cross with Scrooge. Fred says, 'Don't be angry with us, uncle'.

AO1 Clear statement setting out viewpoint

AO2 Close reference to word use and what it means

AO1 Clear progression to next point

AO3 Explains religious context

AO2 Clear link made, with evidence to the structure Dickens uses

AO2 This doesn't add anything, and no analysis

AO2 Relevant idea but not developed sufficiently

Fred's attitude towards people in the novel as a whole is the same as in this passage. As a character who is already kind and thoughtful to others, Fred's character does not change in the book in the same way as Scrooge. Fred says that Christmas is a good time because it is a time when people are 'kind, forgiving, charitable, pleasant' all of which are characteristics that Fred himself possesses. I think that Dickens is saying that this is a good way to behave and how Scrooge behaves is a bad way. Fred often says things like 'God bless it!' and 'God save you!' because he is showing a Christian attitude to other people which the Victorians would have valued.

— Paragraph 4

Later in the book Dickens describes Fred helping the Cratchits when Tiny Tim dies. The connection between Fred and Bob is suggested when Bob reacts by clapping Fred's speech. Later in the book, the Ghost of Christmas Future shows the death of Tiny Tim. Bob tells his wife that Fred has offered to help them and even to get a job for Peter. Mrs Cratchit says he is a 'good soul'. Bob says he believed that Fred 'felt with us' the death of Tim implying that Fred is considerate and has sympathy for other people.

— Paragraph 5

Check the skills

Re-read paragraphs four and five of this response and:

- highlight other **points** made;
- circle any reference to **context**;
- underline any places where the student has made an **interpretation**.

Now you try!

Look again at paragraph three (*The word 'shut-up' links to …*) and improve it by:

- Adding a **topic sentence** that focuses on Fred's attitude towards others in contrast to Scrooge.
- **Explaining** why it is significant to our understanding of Fred that Bob Cratchit **'applauded'** what he said.
- Ending with a **summary point** about the language that Fred uses towards Scrooge and how that conveys Fred's character.
- Improving the overall **style** by making sure your sentences **flow**; using **connectives** to link ideas.

What does a Grade 7+ answer look like?

Read the task again, then the sample answer below.

2. Starting with this extract, explore how Dickens presents Fred's attitudes towards other people.

Write about:

● how Dickens presents Fred's attitudes towards other people in this extract

● how Dickens presents Fred's attitudes towards other people in the novel as a whole. **[30 marks]**

Fred is the first character in the novel that Dickens presents actually conversing with Scrooge. Dickens depicts Fred as not only a character who personifies all the moral values and ideals of the book, but also acts as a direct contrast to his uncle. Previously to this passage, Scrooge has criticised Fred for being 'poor' and has implied he is an 'idiot' for enjoying Christmas, but Fred's speech here provides a counter argument to Scrooge's beliefs. Fred makes an important distinction between things from which he has 'derived good' and things which have 'profited' him in terms of 'gold or silver'. Fred understands the benefits of friendship, whereas Scrooge can only see benefit in financial gain.

Fred values the way Christmas reminds us that we are 'fellow-passengers to the grave' with the metaphor of the shared journey foreshadowing Scrooge's own imminent physical and psychological journey. Dickens's reference to death here reflects Victorian values which included the belief that it was important to be aware of death as part of our journey through life. The theme of death is important in the book as a whole as it reminds Scrooge of the importance of living life well and valuing other people, as Fred does.

Fred's attitude towards other people is reflected in his language. His affectionate use of 'uncle' contrasts with Scrooge's more distant 'sir'. Fred's sincere love for his 'fellow-passengers' is dismissed by Scrooge as rhetorical language that would not be out of place in 'Parliament' – a comment that conveys Scrooge's continual cynicism.

AO1 Clear statement sets out argument

AO2 Immediate structural link made with evidence to earlier part of novel

AO1 Excellent use of embedded quotations brings ideas together

AO2 Carefully selected evidence and detailed analysis of language use and effect

AO3 Excellent knowledge of context linked to Dickens's viewpoint

AO1 Point is developed and interpreted

AO1 Fluent introduction of new aspect to analyse

AO2 Careful choice of quotation and analysis of meaning and effect, using key terms

Another aspect of Fred's attitude towards others is presented by Dickens through Fred's relationship with Bob Cratchit, who here risks his job through the 'impropriety' of applauding Fred's speech. In Stave Four, Fred's compassion is displayed to Scrooge as Fred offers help to the bereaved Cratchit family. Bob's explanation that, 'It really seemed as if he had known our Tiny Tim, and felt with us' suggests that Fred exemplifies the ability to feel empathy, which is something that Dickens feared was missing in the Victorian world of workhouses and treadmills.

— Paragraph 4

Finally, Fred offers Scrooge his ultimate passage to redemption at the end of the novel. Fred's sincere joy at Scrooge's transformation and spending their first family Christmas together is described by Dickens as 'won-der-ful happiness!' with the hyphenated word giving a phonological emphasis to the family's emotions. Furthermore, Dickens uses the term 'wonderful unanimity', meaning 'togetherness' which indicates Fred's ability to unite people, both in a fun way, such as in the party games he so enjoys, and also as friends, family and the wider community.

— Paragraph 5

Check the skills

Re-read paragraphs four and five of this response and:

● highlight any particularly **fluent** or **well-expressed** ideas or key points;

● circle any further references to **context**;

● underline any places where the student has shown **deeper insight** and offered **original** or particularly **thoughtful** ideas or made interesting **links**.

Now you try!

Now, using the plan you made for Question 3 on page 67, write a full response. Here's a reminder of the question:

3. 'Dickens presents the Christmas Ghosts as powerful characters.' Starting with this extract, explore how far you agree with this opinion.

Write about:

● how Dickens presents the Christmas Ghost as a powerful character in this extract

● how Dickens presents the Christmas Ghosts as powerful characters in the novel as a whole. **[30 marks]**

Try to match your answer to the High Level objectives on page 63.

Read this exam-style theme question

Read this extract from Stave Four in which Scrooge is shown his own grave. Then answer the question that follows.

> A churchyard. Here, then, the wretched man whose name he had now to learn, lay underneath the ground. It was a worthy place. Walled in by houses; overrun by grass and weeds, the growth of vegetation's death, not life; choked up with too much burying; fat with repleted appetite. A worthy place!
>
> 5   The Spirit stood among the graves, and pointed down to One. He advanced towards it trembling. The Phantom was exactly as it had been, but he dreaded that he saw new meaning in its solemn shape.
>
> 'Before I draw nearer to that stone to which you point,' said Scrooge, 'answer me one question. Are these the shadows of the things that Will be, or are they
> 10 shadows of things that May be, only.'
>
> Still the Ghost pointed downward to the grave by which it stood.
>
> 'Men's courses will foreshadow certain ends, to which, if persevered in, they must lead,' said Scrooge. 'But if the courses be departed from, the ends will change. Say it is thus with what you show me!'
>
> 15 The Spirit was immovable as ever.
>
> Scrooge crept towards it, trembling as he went; and following the finger, read upon the stone of the neglected grave his own name, EBENEZER SCROOGE.
>
> 'Am I that man who lay upon the bed?' he cried, upon his knees.
>
> The finger pointed from the grave to him, and back again.
>
> 20 'No, Spirit! Oh no, no!'
>
> The finger still was there.
>
> 'Spirit!' he cried, tight clutching at its robe, 'hear me! I am not the man I was. I will not be the man I must have been but for this intercourse. Why show me this, if I am past all hope?'
>
> 25 For the first time the hand appeared to shake.

4. Starting with this extract, explore how Dickens presents death in the novel.

   Write about:
   - how death is presented in this extract
   - how death is presented elsewhere in the novel.

   [30 marks]

NOW read this further theme question

Read this extract from Stave Four in which the thieves are selling the items they have stolen from Scrooge to Old Joe. Then answer the question that follows.

> 'That's your account,' said Joe, 'and I wouldn't give another sixpence, if I was to be boiled for not doing it. Who's next?'
>
> Mrs Dilber was next. Sheets and towels, a little wearing apparel, two old-fashioned silver teaspoons, a pair of sugar-tongs, and a few boots. Her account
> 5 was stated on the wall in the same manner.
>
> 'I always give too much to ladies. It's a weakness of mine, and that's the way I ruin myself,' said old Joe. 'That's your account. If you asked me for another penny, and made it an open question, I'd repent of being so liberal and knock off half-a-crown.'
>
> 10 'And now undo my bundle, Joe,' said the first woman.
>
> Joe went down on his knees for the greater convenience of opening it, and having unfastened a great many knots, dragged out a large and heavy roll of some dark stuff.
>
> 'What do you call this?' said Joe. 'Bed-curtains!'
>
> 15 'Ah!' returned the woman, laughing and leaning forward on her crossed arms. 'Bed-curtains!'
>
> 'You don't mean to say you took 'em down, rings and all, with him lying there?' said Joe.
>
> 'Yes I do,' replied the woman. 'Why not?'
>
> 20 'You were born to make your fortune,' said Joe, 'and you'll certainly do it.

5. Starting with this extract, explore how Dickens presents the ways that avarice affects people's behaviour.

   Write about:

   ● how Dickens presents the ways that avarice affects people's behaviour in this extract

   ● how Dickens presents the ways that avarice affects people's behaviour in the novel as a whole.

   [30 marks]

Five key stages to follow

1. **Read** the **question**; **highlight** key words.
2. **Read** the **passage** with the **key words** from the **question** in mind.
3. Quickly **generate ideas** for your response.
4. **Plan** for paragraphs.
5. **Write** your response; **check it** against your plan as you progress.

What do I focus on?

Highlight the **key words**:

4. Starting with this extract, explore how Dickens presents death in the novel.

   Write about:

   ● how death is presented in this extract
   ● how death is presented elsewhere in the novel

What do they tell you? Focus on both extract and whole text; explain what specific methods Dickens uses; stick to death as the main topic.

How should I read the passage?

● Check for any immediate links to the question (e.g. Scrooge's grave).
● Look for any evidence/quotations you could highlight (e.g. he is as **'choked up with too much burying'**, **'He advanced towards it trembling'**).

How do I get my ideas?

Note your ideas in a spider diagram or list them in a table:

The extract

The churchyard 'overgrown by weeds'

'The Phantom' is a figure of death

'I am not the man I was.'

'The kind hand trembled': the Ghost feels sorry for Scrooge

How Death is presented

The novel as a whole

Marley's death: 'dead as a door-nail', humour + horror of his punishment after death

Scrooge wants poor to die: 'decrease the surplus population'

Stave Four: death of Tiny Tim as key turning point

The extract	The novel as a whole
• Churchyard 'overgrown by weeds' • 'The Phantom' is a figure of death • Death makes him want to change: 'I am not the man I was.' • 'The kind hand trembled': the Ghost feels sorry for Scrooge	• Marley's death: 'dead as a door-nail', humour+ horror of his punishment after death • Scrooge wants poor to die: 'decrease the surplus population' • Death of Tiny Tim

HOW do I structure my ideas?

Make a **plan** for **paragraphs**.* Decide the order for your points:

- Paragraph 1: Go straight into your first point: *The overgrown churchyard reflects Scrooge's isolation; Victorian context of death.*
- Paragraph 2: The Phantom represents death: *ultimate persuasion for Scrooge to change.*
- Paragraph 3: *Contrast with the more humorous elements of Marley's death, but link to Marley's punishment after death.*
- Paragraph 4: *Description of death of Tim/debtor family.*
- Paragraph 5: *Scrooge's redemption after facing death. Embraces life:* **'I will live in the Past, the Present, and the Future.'**

HOW do I write effectively?

Write **clear**, **analytical** paragraphs and **embed** your evidence fluently, e.g.:

In the extract, Dickens presents a lonely death as the ultimate fate for Scrooge and which Scrooge must confront in order for him to change. Dickens creates tension by withholding from Scrooge the name of the 'wretched' man, 'whose name he had now to learn'. Throughout Stave Four, Scrooge has watched in horror as people have reacted to the man's death with a mixture of indifference and pleasure which makes the revelation so shocking, 'No, Spirit! Oh, no, no!', and secures Scrooge's determination to change.

- Overview point – extract
- Key term
- Quotation embedded in the sentence
- Link to rest of key focus of question
- Link to rest of novel

Now you try!

Re-read Question 5 on page 73 and plan your response in the same way.

* The plan above and the sample answers on pages 76 and 78 have five paragraphs, but you don't need to be limited to this if you have more points to include (and time to write them!).

75

EXAM PRACTICE Grade 5 annotated sample answer

What does a Grade 5 answer look like?

Read the task again, then the sample answer below.

4. Starting with this extract, explore how Dickens presents death in the novel.

Write about:
- how death is presented in this extract
- how death is presented elsewhere in the novel. **[30 marks]**

In the passage Scrooge is made to face his own death having observed how other people have reacted to his death. Dickens creates a sinister atmosphere by describing an overgrown cemetery that is 'choked up with too much burying' which may have reflected some of the state of Victorian cemeteries at that time, but is also symbolic of Scrooge's isolation and separation from society. Having a well-tended grave and a well-attended funeral was a Victorian ideal of death as this would reflect a person's success in life and Scrooge reacts with horror, as would any Victorian gentleman, to this undignified ending.

> **AO1** Clear statement setting out viewpoint
>
> **AO2** Close reference to word use and what it means
>
> **AO3** A point of context

Scrooge is terrified to look at the grave and Dickens describes him 'trembling' as he approaches it. This contrasts with the arrogant Scrooge who accuses Marley of being created by an 'undigested bit of beef' and was disbelieving of the power of ghosts in Stave One. When Scrooge asks if what he sees are 'Shadows' of what 'may be', the modal verb 'may' shows that Scrooge is hoping he can change the future.

> **AO2** Clear link made, with evidence to structure used by Dickens

Throughout the novel, Scrooge gradually develops emotional reactions to the people and events around him. This is important for Scrooge's transformation. You can tell that Scrooge is frightened in this scene when it says 'Spirit! He cried, still clutching tight at its robe. The grave is described as 'neglected', which shows no one has cared for it. Scrooge then walks up to the grave and reads his name, 'EBENEZER SCROOGE', written in capital letters.

> **AO2** Explains quotation but doesn't develop sufficiently
>
> **AO2** This doesn't add anything, and no analysis

76

The Ghost of Christmas Future is different from the other ghosts as it appears to be similar to the personification of death in the 'Grim Reaper' that would have been familiar to the Victorians. It has a 'spectral hand' and is described as a 'heap of black' at the beginning of Stave Four and it does not speak, suggesting that it is not possible to communicate or bargain with Death. Its 'solemn shape' fills Scrooge with dread and the adjective 'immovable' suggests its immense power. However, Dickens describes the ghost's hand as appearing 'to shake' which does suggest the ghost has some sympathy for Scrooge's terror and gives a more human quality to the ghost.

— Paragraph 4

Overall, this extract presents death in a gothic and terrifying way. However, in contrast, elsewhere in the novel death is presented with a different tone. Dickens uses dark humour in the presentation of the business men who discuss Scrooge's death, each of whom have a slightly funny aspect in their appearance such as a 'monstrous chin' and a 'pendulous excrescence' and who joke about eating lunch at the funeral. The debtor family who are relieved by the death of Scrooge have 'a happier house for this man's death' and the scene has a gentle, domestic tone.

— Paragraph 5

Check the skills

Re-read paragraphs four and five of this response and:
- highlight other **points** made;
- circle any reference to **context**;
- underline any places where the student has made an **interpretation**.

Now you try!

Look again at paragraph three ('Throughout the novel …') and improve it by:
- Adding a **reference or quotation** about Scrooge from earlier in the book to provide further evidence of Scrooge's developing emotions.
- **Explaining** why it is significant that the grave is **'neglected'**.
- Ending with a **summary point** about death and how this has been a key idea through the novel.
- Improving the overall **style** by making sure your sentences **flow**; using **connectives** to link ideas.

What does a Grade 7+ answer look like?

Read the task again, then the sample answer below.

4. Starting with this extract, explore how Dickens presents death in the novel.

Write about:

- how death is presented in this extract
- how death is presented elsewhere in the novel. **[30 marks]**

Dickens presents Death as a constant presence throughout the novel, right from the opening line, 'Marley was dead: to begin with', and this passage is the culmination of these various presentations of it. Throughout Stave Four, Dickens has increased the dramatic tension as Scrooge is made to observe different reactions to the death of an unnamed man, finally arriving at 'A Churchyard.' with the brief nominal sentence conveying the significance of the location.

AO1 Clear statement sets out argument

AO2 Immediate structural link made with evidence to earlier part of novel

AO1 Author's technique explained

Dickens's descriptions of the churchyard and Scrooge's terror convey the importance of the scene as the final message from the Ghosts to Scrooge. The fact that this man has been buried in a 'neglected' place, which is 'choked up with too much burying' reflects his position as an outcast from normal society, which for the Victorians would have involved having a well-tended grave. The comment 'A worthy place!' conveys a dark irony that this grave conveys no worth at all.

AO3 Comment on context of death

In the extract, Death is personified through the Ghost himself with connotations of the mythic Grim Reaper, presenting death as a silent, terrible force which merely points to 'the One', with the capitalisation conveying the significance of that particular gravestone. Scrooge does not use the word 'death' as he questions the Ghost, but instead uses euphemisms such as 'the shadows' and 'certain ends' to avoid saying the word that holds so much fear for him. Dickens depicts Scrooge confronting his own gravestone in a state of terror. He 'crept' towards it, with the verb conveying his reluctance and he stays 'upon his knees' as he looks to the Ghost for confirmation, which implies Scrooge's powerlessness.

AO1 Point is developed and interpreted

AO3 Reference to context fluently made

AO1 Developed comment

AO2 Perceptive interpretation of language and content

As mentioned earlier, the book opens with the reference to Marley's death. Dickens uses the first person omniscient voice to explain that the death must be 'distinctly understood' as real and makes a literary connection to the death of Hamlet's father as another text that depends on the literal existence of ghosts for its dramatic impact. Scrooge's avarice is conveyed by a reference to how he saved money when arranging the funeral with 'an undoubted bargain'. This connection between the themes of money and death is continued throughout the book.

Paragraph 4

Finally, my view is that the pivotal 'death' of Tiny Tim arguably has a greater impact on Scrooge than any other event and is that which forces Scrooge to accept responsibility for the effect of his treatment of others. The description of Bob as, 'He broke down, all at once. He couldn't help it' uses simple monosyllabic language and a contraction 'couldn't' to plainly show Bob's devastation. This 'death' is referenced in the final pages and leaves the reader with the image of the redeemed Scrooge now a 'second father' to Tim, rather than a mourner.

Paragraph 5

Check the skills

Re-read paragraphs four and five of this response and:

- highlight any particularly **fluent** or **well-expressed** ideas or key points;
- circle any further references to **context**;
- underline any places where the student has shown **deeper insight** and offered **original** or particularly **thoughtful** ideas or made interesting **links**.

Now you try!

Now, using the plan you made for Question 5 on page 75, write a full response. Here's a reminder of the question:

5. Starting with this extract, explore how Dickens presents the ways that avarice affects people's behaviour?

Write about:

- how Dickens presents the ways that avarice affects people's behaviour in this extract
- how Dickens presents the ways that avarice affects people's behaviour in the novel as a whole. **[30 marks]**

Try to match your answer to the High Level objectives on page 63.

79

Now you try!

Now, practise applying the skills you have learned to these two new questions. In each case:

● Note down key points from the extract.

● Select the key quotations you want to use from the extract.

● Repeat the process with other ideas from the novel as a whole.

● Write your answer.

● Look at the suggested list of key points you could have made for each question in the **Answers** (page 88).

Read this extract from Stave Four in which Scrooge is shown his own grave. Then answer the question that follows.

> 'Merry Christmas to us all, my dears. God bless us!'
> Which all the family re-echoed.
> 'God bless us every one!' said Tiny Tim, the last of all.
> He sat very close to his father's side upon his little stool. Bob held his
> 5   withered little hand in his, as if he loved the child, and wished to keep him by
> his side, and dreaded that he might be taken from him.
>   'Spirit,' said Scrooge, with an interest he had never felt before, 'tell me if Tiny
> Tim will live.'
>   'I see a vacant seat,' replied the Ghost, 'in the poor chimney corner, and
> 10   a crutch without an owner, carefully preserved. If these shadows remain
> unaltered by the Future, the child will die.'
>   'No, no,' said Scrooge. 'Oh, no, kind Spirit! say he will be spared.'
>   'If these shadows remain unaltered by the Future, none other of my race,'
> returned the Ghost, 'will find him here. What then? If he be like to die, he had
> 15   better do it, and decrease the surplus population.'

6. 'The relationship between Scrooge and Tiny Tim is an essential part of the book'. To what extent do you agree with this statement?

Write about:

● the relationship between Scrooge and Tiny Tim in this extract

● the relationship between Scrooge and Tiny Tim in the novel as a whole.

[30 marks]

Read this extract from Stave Three in which the Cratchit family are gathering together on Christmas Day. Then answer the question that follows.

> 'What has ever got your precious father then,' said Mrs Cratchit. 'And your brother, Tiny Tim; and Martha warn't as late last Christmas Day by half-an-hour!'
>
> 'Here's Martha, mother!' said a girl, appearing as she spoke.
>
> 5   'Here's Martha, mother!' cried the two young Cratchits. 'Hurrah! There's such a goose, Martha!'
>
> 'Why, bless your heart alive, my dear, how late you are!' said Mrs Cratchit, kissing her a dozen times, and taking off her shawl and bonnet for her with officious zeal.
>
> 10   'We'd a deal of work to finish up last night,' replied the girl, 'and had to clear away this morning, mother!'
>
> 'Well! Never mind so long as you are come,' said Mrs Cratchit. 'Sit ye down before the fire, my dear, and have a warm, Lord bless ye!'
>
> 'No, no! There's father coming,' cried the two young Cratchits, who were
>
> 15 everywhere at once. 'Hide Martha, hide!'
>
> So Martha hid herself, and in came little Bob, the father, with at least three feet of comforter exclusive of the fringe, hanging down before him; and his threadbare clothes darned up and brushed, to look seasonable; and Tiny Tim upon his shoulder. Alas for Tiny Tim, he bore a little crutch, and had his limbs
>
> 20 supported by an iron frame!

7. Starting with this extract, how does Dickens present the importance of family?

Write about:

● how Dickens presents the family in this extract

● how Dickens presents families in the novel as a whole.

[30 marks]

GLOSSARY

Literary or language terms	Explanation
adjective	a word used to describe something or somebody (e.g. the *red* hat)
archetype	a typical example of a kind of person
climax	the highpoint of a play, act or story
connective	a link between paragraphs, showing the relationship between them
counterpoint	a character that is an opposite to another character
dialogue	speech and conversation between characters
embedded quotation	a quotation in the middle of a sentence of analysis
epiphany	a moment of great understanding or realisation
foregrounded	a literary term used to point to a feature of the text that is emphasised
foreshadowing	a hint of what is to come in a work of literature
form	the type of text the writer is using, such as a speech, letter, prayer, short story, novel
genre	a type of text that will have particular features and content, such as a ghost story, a thriller, romance
Gothic	in literature a style that includes horror, the supernatural, romance and death
hyperbole	a description that is exaggerated for a particular effect
imagery	descriptive language that uses images to make actions, objects and characters more vivid in the reader's mind
irony	deliberately saying one thing that has a secondary meaning to create humour or to show an opinion
literal	language that describes something that is true or actual
metaphor	when one thing is used to describe another to create a striking or unusual image
mood	the **tone** or atmosphere created by an artistic work
narrator	the **voice** or person that tells the story in a novel or poem
noun	a word that denotes an object
novel	a fictional narrative of considerable length
novella	narrative **prose** longer than a short story, but shorter than a **novel**
onomatopoeia	a word that suggests its meaning through its sound (e.g. 'meow', 'squelch')
pathetic fallacy	a technique that suggests that the weather is reflecting a character's **mood**
personification	the treatment or description of an object or idea as though it is human with human feelings and attributes
phrase	a part of a sentence that does not contain a **verb**, and may be a familiar saying
plot	the main events in a novel or short story
preface	a very brief introduction to a novel that may explain a key idea or inspiration behind the story
prose	the natural flow of speech used in novels and other works, unlike poetry which has a more rhythmic structure
repetition	repeated words or patterns
resolution	the end of a story that generally ties its different elements together
simile	when one thing is compared directly with another using 'like' or 'as'
slang	everyday, informal words
symbol	something that represents something else, usually with meanings that are widely known (e.g. a dove as a symbol of peace)
theme	an idea running through a work of literature or art
tone	See **mood**
topic sentence	a sentence that expresses the main idea of a paragraph, sometimes the first of the paragraph
verb	a word that denotes an action (e.g. she *sang* loudly)
vocabulary	the choice of words used by a writer
voice	the speaker or **narrator** of a poem or work of fiction. This persona is created in the speaker's mind, though sometimes it can seem close to the poet's or writer's own voice

ANSWERS

Stave 1 – Now you try! (page 7)

Fred and Scrooge have very different attitudes towards Christmas. Fred's attitude is positive, not just towards the party games that he is later shown enjoying, but also on a spiritual basis. Fred values Christmas as a time, 'when men and women seem by one consent to open their shut-up hearts freely'. The phrase 'by one consent' conveys the sense that Christmas brings people together, in direct contrast to the solitary life led by Scrooge.

Stave 2 – Now you try! (page 9)

Dickens continues to develop the presentation of character in Stave Two. An important aspect of Scrooge's character is revealed when Scrooge cries, which Dickens implies through an open question: 'Why did his cold eye glisten, and his heart leap up as they went past?' Scrooge is normally 'cold' which signifies lacking emotions, but the verb 'glisten' suggests tears. Furthermore, the verb 'leap up' conveys strong and sudden feelings on seeing his old school friends.

Stave 3 – Now you try! (page 11)

Another function of Stave Three is to explore the effects of poverty. Dickens presents the children 'Ignorance and Want' that live under the skirts of the Ghost, portraying the idea that poverty is always just underneath the surface. Poverty is shockingly personified as degrading and inhuman, with children suffering the most; Dickens uses a list of emotive adjectives 'wretched, abject, frightful, hideous, miserable' to convey the effects that poverty and lack of education have on children.

Stave 4 – Now you try! (page 13)

Stave Four presents different characters' thoughts and feelings about each other. An important aspect of strong emotion is explored when Scrooge witnesses the Cratchit family's reaction to Tiny Tim's death. Bob's feelings are shown in the repetition of the word 'little' which emphasises Tiny Tim's fragility and vulnerability. The verb 'cried' shows Bob, for the first time, showing negative emotions, when he has always faced the hardships of life with calm and acceptance.

Stave 5 – Now you try! (page 15)

Dickens deliberately changes the weather in Stave Five to reflect the change in Scrooge. The wintry weather is now described as 'No fog, no mist; clear, bright, jovial, stirring, cold'. The clearing fog is a metaphor for the new clarity that Scrooge has. Dickens personifies the weather as 'jovial', which means 'jolly', making a further link between the weather and Scrooge's mood.

Form and structure (page 17)

Dickens uses a clear narrative voice in the novel to imply that the story is being read out loud to us.

The narrative voice sometimes makes first-person comments, such as 'Scrooge and he were partners for I don't know how many years', using a contraction 'don't' to suggest that someone who actually knows Scrooge is talking. This makes the story of 'A Christmas Carol' more believable, despite its supernatural form and unusual structure.

Quick revision – Quick quiz (pages 18–19)

1. Marley. 2. Fred comes to wish Scrooge a merry Christmas. 3. Scrooge believes the poor do not deserve any more help. 4. Marley is weighed down by chains and money boxes. 5. Scrooge's school. 6. Fan has died. 7. Fezziwig holds the party to thank his workers at Christmas. 8. Belle breaks off the engagement because of Scrooge's obsession with money. 9. The Ghost is surrounded by Christmas food. 10. The families have their dinner cooked at the bakers. 11. Four. 12. They are Tiny Tim's siblings. 13. Want and Ignorance. 14. Black. 15. Scrooge. 16. Three. 17. Fred. 18. A new person is working there. 19. Scrooge hears Christmas bells. 20. No.

Quick revision – Power paragraphs (page 19)

- When we first meet Scrooge, although he is indoors, he is described as 'blue' as the 'cold within him froze his features' which conveys his lack of emotion and unkind behaviour. Fred, in contrast, is described as 'ruddy' which means 'red' and suggests warmth. Fred is excited about Christmas and is 'merry', whereas Scrooge says anyone who celebrates Christmas is an 'idiot'. Fred is cheerful and ignores Scrooge's unkind words.
- When Scrooge is able to see himself as a young child, Dickens says his eye begins to 'glisten' and he is moved to shout in 'ecstasy' at one of his memories. This contrasts with the cold and detached Scrooge at the start of the novel. The reader sees the Ghost is affecting Scrooge's behaviour. Scrooge can also see himself as a lonely child which causes him to feel sympathy, an emotion he rarely feels.

Quick revision – Exam practice (page 19)

- Dickens structures the text to place the moment of revelation when Scrooge sees his gravestone at the end of Stave Four. 'Scrooge crept towards it', the verb 'crept' creating tension and showing Scrooge's fear. Scrooge now understands that he will suffer the consequences of his behaviour but he has a final chance to change.
- Scrooge says he 'will honour Christmas in my heart' because he understands the Ghost's message, and he promises that the Spirits will 'thrive' within him as he keeps their moral message alive. Dickens uses Christmas to symbolise kind behaviour and taking responsibility for others around you.

ANSWERS

SETTINGS AND CONTEXT

Victorian society – Now you try! (page 21)

Conditions faced by the Victorian urban poor are explored by Dickens through the descriptions of London in the novel. For example, we see a homeless family in the first Stave, 'a wretched woman with an infant … upon a door-step'. The adjective 'wretched' conveys a sense of desperation. They are watched by the ghosts of London who are tortured by missing their chance to help the poor when they were alive.

Christmas and morality – Now you try! (page 23)

Dickens presents Fred as a character who embodies the spirit of Christmas when he explains to Scrooge the importance of Christmas as a time when people 'open their shut-up hearts'. This is the opposite of Scrooge who is self-contained like an 'oyster'. Christmas, according to Dickens, is about sharing the holiday time with others, whether it is family, or fellow workers, like the sailors and lighthouse men that Scrooge observes, or just people in the street.

Quick revision – Quick quiz (page 25)

1. The workhouses fed and housed the poor who could not work. 2. Poor families had to send children out to work. 3. They went to the cities to work in the new factories. 4. Fezziwig's warehouse, the ship, the mine, the lighthouse. 5. Christianity. 6. Cold. 7. People could sell stolen items. 8. Christmas. 9. The people working in finance in the city or 'Change. 10. Marley's Ghost.

Quick revision – Power paragraphs (page 25)

- Dickens uses the setting of Old Joe's den in a 'foul and narrow' part of town to reflect the horrific effects of poverty. The setting shocks Scrooge because he has not seen it close up before.
- The theme of poverty is developed as Joe's den is connected to crime. Mrs Dilber says 'Every person has a right to take care of themselves. He always did!' implying that their stealing is no worse than Scrooge's own grasping behaviour.

CHARACTERS

Scrooge (Staves 1–3) – Now you try! (page 27)

Dickens explores Scrooge's changing character through his failed engagement with Belle. Belle ends their engagement because she has been 'displaced' by an 'idol'. An idol is something you worship. In this case it is money and 'gain', which Belle calls Scrooge's 'master-passion'. Belle can see this is the 'greedy, restless motion' in Scrooge's eye. This may 'torture' Scrooge, but is an essential lesson in how greed destroys happiness.

Scrooge (Staves 4–5) – Now you try! (page 29)

Dickens shows how Scrooge's behaviour becomes much kinder through the description of Scrooge's relationship with Tiny Tim, who Dickens emphatically explains 'did NOT die' and to whom Scrooge becomes

a 'second father'. This metaphorical role for Scrooge conveys to the reader Scrooge's new-found ability to take responsibility for another person and his continued redemption through his fatherly role.

Marley's Ghost – Now you try! (page 31)

As Scrooge's deceased partner, Marley's Ghost is used by Dickens to introduce Scrooge to the idea of being punished for your actions in the afterlife. Marley's 'chain' is purely of his own making, and he tells Scrooge that Scrooge's own chain will be even longer and heavier. The chain symbolises how every time Marley was greedy or ignored a chance to help other people a new link was 'forged', increasing Marley's Ghost's pain.

The Ghost of Christmas Yet to Come – Now you try! (page 33)

The Ghost of Christmas Yet to Come does not speak to Scrooge, but it does respond when, at the graveside, Scrooge reacts with terror at the sight of his own gravestone and begs the Ghost that he might alter 'the shadows' that the Ghost has shown him. Dickens explains that the 'kind hand trembled' with the verb 'trembled' implying the Ghost's own strong emotion as it sympathises with Scrooge. You could argue that this empathy is the final push that Scrooge needs to change.

The Cratchits – Now you try! (page 35)

The relationship between Scrooge and Bob conveys a great deal about their characters. Through the way Scrooge treats Bob at work, Dickens shows one of the worst aspects of Scrooge, as he threatens Bob will 'lose his situation' for taking Christmas day as holiday. This could have put most of the Cratchits in the workhouse and so conveys Scrooge's cruel and heartless manner. Bob, in contrast, refuses to criticise Scrooge, in a similar way to the kind and forgiving Fred.

Fan – Now you try! (page 37)

As Scrooge's little sister, Dickens uses Fan to show that Scrooge's childhood was not always easy. It is through Fan's words that we learn that their father is 'so much kinder than he used to be' implying that the young Scrooge had suffered some cruelty at his father's hands. It is Fan who comes to visit Scrooge, rather than his parents, reflecting Dickens's own difficult relationship with his parents.

Belle – Now you try! (page 39)

As Scrooge's former fiancée and only sweetheart, Belle is the first person to notice the effect that the love of money has on Scrooge. She refers to his 'nobler passions' which Dickens does not explain further, but there is an implication that Scrooge once cared about other things rather than money, but which 'fall away' as Scrooge spends more and more time on making money.

Quick revision – Quick quiz (pages 40–1)

1. Scrooge. 2. Fred. 3. Bob Cratchit. 4. Scrooge's doorknocker. 5. Scrooge. 6. The headmaster. 7. The Ghost of Christmas Past. 8. Green 9. Over 1800.

10. Fifteen. 11. Apprentice milliner. 12. Scrooge. 13. The Ghost of Christmas Present. 14. Fred. 15. Scrooge. 16. Old Joe. 17. Laundress (she washes clothes). 18. They have more time to pay back their debt. 19. Scrooge. 20. Nearly twenty minutes.

Quick revision – Power paragraphs (page 41)

1. The Ghost of Christmas Past reminds Scrooge of his childhood and younger days, something which he seems to have forgotten about, when you see his amazed reactions as he 'rejoiced beyond all bounds to see them'. Dickens presents Scrooge feeling strong emotions of 'ecstasy' and he is described as 'heightened and excited' suggesting that the Ghost is encouraging Scrooge to engage with the world around him, rather than shutting it out.
2. The Cratchits represent Dickens's ideal family. Despite their poverty and ill health, they are kind and gentle to each other and are always happy to be together; Mrs Cratchit kisses her daughter 'a dozen times' when she arrives on Christmas Day, for example. Scrooge's unkindness casts 'a dark shadow' over the Cratchits' Christmas Day, but he is eventually redeemed by becoming a 'second father' to Tiny Tim.

Quick revision – Exam practice (page 41)

- Dickens presents Belle as gentle, who is quick to smile at her husband, 'laughing as he laughed'. Belle's daughter leans 'fondly' on her father, 'graceful and full of promise'. They are an ideal family unit, making Scrooge's sight grow 'very dim' as tears fill his eyes.
- Scrooge, in contrast, is mean and unkind. He scorns Fred's love for his wife as 'ridiculous'. Scrooge implies he will see Fred 'in that extremity' (Hell) before he would have dinner with him, having forgotten how close he was to Fred's mother, Fan, as a child.

THEMES

Christmas – Now you try! (page 43)

Dickens presents the images of Ignorance and Want to remind the reader that poverty still exists at Christmas, as the charity collectors reminded Scrooge: 'a time, of all others, when Want is keenly felt, and Abundance rejoices'. The two wolf-like children revealed by the Ghost of Christmas Present symbolise the desperate plight of the Victorian poor and contrast with the celebrations earlier in the Stave.

Responsibility – Now you try! (page 45)

Dickens shows that Scrooge has an opportunity for taking personal responsibility by helping the Cratchits and not expecting the church or the state to provide help. He does so by, by paying Bob a fair salary. Helping a 'struggling family' when it is easily within Scrooge's ability not only improves the family's life, it also prevents the untimely death of Tiny Tim, and makes Scrooge himself a happier person.

Change and redemption – Now you try! (page 47)

Dickens shows that redemption is only possible when Scrooge fully understands the consequences of his decisions. The agent for that is the final Spirit who so terrifies Scrooge that he says 'I hope to live to be another man from what I was'. Scrooge's use of the verb 'hope' suggests that he is now in mortal fear, but that he understands that redemption will come only if he can be 'another man'.

Money and avarice – Now you try! (page 49)

Dickens presents Scrooge's final lesson about the effects of avarice when the Ghost of Christmas Yet to Come shows Scrooge his own dead body, stripped even of its shirt by the thieves. Although Scrooge has not accepted the body is actually his, he can see the horror of being reduced to this state by 'avarice' and 'griping cares'. The adjective 'griping' suggests that his greed clutches him in a painful grip.

Poverty and education – Now you try! (page 51)

Dickens conveys the plight of the poor when the charity collectors visit and explain that 'hundreds of thousands are in want of common comforts'. The phrase 'common comforts' means that these people are so poor that they are not able to afford food, clothing and heating. Scrooge, however, believes that this is just making 'idle people merry' which was a common argument supporting the workhouses of the time.

Family – Now you try! (page 53)

Dickens regularly reminds the reader that Scrooge actually has a loving family. The first visitor to his office is Fred, who responds to Scrooge's rudeness with 'Don't be angry, uncle', reminding Scrooge of their connection. Fred later explains he 'means to give him [Scrooge] the same chance every year'. When Scrooge finally visits Fred in Stave Five, Fred nearly shakes his 'arm off' in happiness.

Quick revision – Quick quiz (pages 54–5)

1. The Cratchits. 2. Fred's. 3. Scrooge sends the turkey by a cab (carriage). 4. Bells. 5. Jacob Marley. 6. The ghosts of London. 7. Fan. 8. The Ghost of Christmas Past. 9. Scrooge buys another 'coal-scuttle' to make it warmer. 10. Tiny Tim will die. 11. Scrooge ties himself up in knots in his excitement. 12. It grows older. 13. Stone. 14. One. 15. Bob Cratchit. 16. Peter Cratchit. 17. Ignorance is worse because without education children will never leave poverty. 18. Scrooge. 19. Bob, Martha and Peter. 20. One.

Quick revision – Power paragraphs (page 55)

1. Marley's Ghost shows responsibility for Scrooge's well-being by giving him a 'chance and hope of escaping my fate'. Marley describes the punishment of not taking responsibility – 'doomed to wander through the world' – and the 'ponderous chain' that Scrooge himself carries. He finishes with showing Scrooge the other ghosts who are also tortured for their lack of kindness and responsibility to the poor of London.

2. Fred shows unconditional family love for Scrooge: he has resolved to wish Scrooge 'merry Christmas' every year, he shows 'laughter and good-humour' to his family, he arranges parties, feasts and games, is shown to help the Cratchits on the death of Tiny Tim, and welcomes Scrooge happily into the family at the end of the novel.

Quick revision – Exam practice (page 55)

- Scrooge lives in a small apartment with only one bedroom, even though he is rich. He has a 'small fire' though it is a 'bitter night' and he eats 'gruel' which is a thin soup that normally only poor people would eat out of desperation. Scrooge will not burn more candles even though he is frightened, declaring that 'darkness is cheap'.
- Scrooge refuses to heat the office and keeps the coal locked in his room. He uses a simile to say Bob that they will need 'to part' (Bob will lose his job) if he tries to get more coal. Scrooge threatens the carol singer with a ruler rather than rewarding him for singing. He complains Bob is 'picking' his 'pocket' for having paid leave on Christmas Day.

LANGUAGE

Imagery and vocabulary – Now you try! (page 57)
Scrooge's description of himself at the end of the novel shows how much he has changed. He uses a simile to say he is 'as light as a feather'. This simile conveys his relief that he has survived his encounter with the Ghosts, the last of which left him 'sobbing violently'. Dickens uses this simile to suggest that Scrooge has now set himself free from the greed and isolation that has weighed him down.

Narrative style and voice – Now you try! (page 59)
Scrooge's way of talking throughout the novel reflects his gradual change in personality. In Stave One his dialogue conveys his rude and aggressive manner. He insults Fred by calling him 'poor enough' and then dismisses him and ignores Fred's Christmas invitation by repeatedly saying 'Good afternoon' to whatever Fred says. Although 'Good afternoon' in itself is not a rude phrase, to say it so repeatedly makes it unpleasant and is typical of Dickens's detailed style.

Quick revision – Quick quiz (page 61)
1. Ignorance and Want. 2. Personification. 3. A lie. 4. The list emphasises the avarice in Marley's life. 5. 'Strong' and 'hearty'. 6. Scratch suggests being uncomfortable/unpleasant. 7. Fezziwig. 8. First person. 9. Excitement/wonder. 10. Secretive behaviour.

Quick revision – Power paragraphs (page 61)
- Dickens uses a simile to describe the face of Marley's Ghost in the doorknocker glowing 'like a bad lobster in a dark cellar'. This implies that Marley is rotten and his appearance is unwelcome. Adjectives 'perfectly motionless' and 'frightful' convey the Ghost's menacing nature.

- The image of Marley's Ghost's jaw' dropping on his chest creates an atmosphere of fright and humour at the same time. Marley addresses Scrooge by his full name, 'Ebenezer Scrooge', showing his power over Scrooge.

EXAM PRACTICE

Planning your character response – Now you try! (page 67)
- Paragraph 1: The Ghost is physically big, of gigantic size', and commands Scrooge, who is described as timid
- Paragraph 2: Power is shown through age/sword/confidence – 'jolly Giant'/size of family – 'eighteen hundred' brothers
- Paragraph 3: The Ghost of Christmas Past can seem childlike, of a 'child's proportions', but is strong and can travel in time
- Paragraph 4: Ghost of Christmas Future is a 'quiet and dark' figure of death which has the ultimate power to show the future and gives Scrooge the final chance to change
- Paragraph 5: The Ghosts are the main factors in Scrooge's change; can stop and change time, make him face himself, 'again Scrooge saw himself', and teach him empathy and kindness

Grade 5 sample answer – Check the skills (page 69)
- Points: Fred's attitude towards people in the novel as a whole is the same as in this passage. As a character who is already kind and thoughtful to others, Fred's character does not change in the same way as Scrooge. Later in the novel Dickens describes Fred helping the Cratchits when Tiny Tim dies. The connection between Fred and Bob is suggested when Bob reacts by clapping Fred's speech.
- Context: Fred is showing a Christian attitude to other people which the Victorians would have valued.
- Interpretation: Fred says that Christmas is a good time because it is a time when people are 'kind, forgiving, charitable, pleasant' all of which are characteristics that Fred himself possesses. Bob says he believed that Fred 'felt with us' the death of Tim implying that Fred is considerate and has sympathy for other.

Grade 5 sample answer – Now you try! (page 69)
The descriptions of Scrooge clearly convey how different he is in character from Fred. For example, the word 'shut-up', which links to Dickens's descriptions of Scrooge as 'self-contained' in an earlier Stave, develops the contrast between the two characters' attitudes towards other people. Fred's attitude to other people is that they are 'fellow-passengers' showing that he believes in being part of a community with each other. Bob Cratchit 'applauded' in agreement with Fred when Fred praises Christmas, conveying a sense of community and implying a connection between Fred and Bob that will be referred to again later in the

novel. Furthermore, Fred's friendly attitude to all even encompasses Scrooge, with Fred's comment, 'Don't be angry with us, uncle' conveying his patience and even affection for his uncle.

Grade 7+ sample answer – Check the skills (page 71)

- Points: Fred's attitude towards others is presented by Dickens through Fred's relationship with Bob Cratchit. Fred's compassion is displayed to Scrooge as Fred offers help to the bereaved Cratchit family. Fred offers Scrooge his ultimate passage to redemption at the end of the novel.
- Context: Fred exemplifies the ability to feel empathy, which is something that Dickens feared was missing in the Victorian world of workhouses and treadmills.
- Interpretation: Dickens uses the term 'wonderful unanimity', meaning 'togetherness', which indicates Fred's ability to unite people, both in a fun way, such as in the party games he so enjoys, and also as friends, family and the wider community.

Grade 7+ sample answer – Now you try! (page 71)

AO1

- The power of the Ghost frightens Scrooge and this is a factor in his transformation.
- The Ghost can command Scrooge: 'Look upon me!'
- The Ghost appears physically strong and confident: 'its unconstrained demeanour'.
- The Ghosts have the power to move backwards and forwards in Scrooge's life.

AO2

- Adverbs reflect Scrooge's fear of the Ghost's power: 'timidly', 'submissively'.
- Ancient strength is implied through the image of the 'antique scabbard'.
- The Ghost of Christmas Future shows its power through its 'immovability' and 'mysterious presence'.
- Dickens's use of the structure allows the power of the Ghosts to develop: from the mild Ghost of Christmas Past, the genial Ghost of Christmas Present to the terrifying death-like Ghost of Christmas Future.

AO3

- Victorian interest in the power of ghosts and the afterlife would have made this story seem particularly relevant and contemporary.
- The symbolic power of the supernatural links to Victorian attitudes to Christmas and the poor. Dickens uses the supernatural throughout the novel, for example with the revelation of 'Ignorance and Want' beneath the Ghost's robes, to make a strong social comment that both feasting and poverty are present at Christmas time and readers should be aware of the presence of both.

Planning your theme response – Now you try! (page 75)

- Paragraph 1: All the characters in the scene are focused on making as much money as possible. Joe says he would rather be 'boiled' than pay out more money and would 'knock off half a crown' if they asked for more.
- Paragraph 2: The avarice is shown through the theft of trivial items such as 'sheets and towels' and 'a pair of sugar tongs' as everything is seen as a financial commodity.
- Paragraph 3: The unwrapping of the curtains is described in detail to build up to the full horror of what avarice has driven the charwoman to do: steal Scrooge's bed curtains 'with him lying there'.
- Paragraph 4: Avarice alters the young Scrooge: his face 'had begun to wear the signs of avarice'. It causes his relationship with Belle to end.

Grade 5 sample answer – Check the skills (page 77)

- Points: The Ghost of Christmas Future is different from the other ghosts as it appears to be similar to the personification of death. However, Dickens gives a more human quality to the ghost. Dickens uses dark humour in the presentation of the business men who discuss Scrooge's death.
- Context: The 'Grim Reaper' would have been familiar to the Victorians.
- Interpretation: It is not possible to communicate or bargain with Death. The adjective 'immovable' suggests its immense power. This extract presents death in a gothic and terrifying way

Grade 5 sample answer – Now you try! (page 77)

Throughout the novel, Scrooge has gradually developed emotional reactions to the people and events around him, such as the 'strangest agitation' he feels as he watches Fezziwig's Christmas party. This begins Scrooge's journey to developing understanding and compassion towards other people. In Victorian times it was considered important to tend graves, but Scrooge's grave is described as 'neglected', implying Scrooge's complete isolation. The continuous verb 'clutching' depicts Scrooge's great fear as he begs the spirit to allow him a chance to change. Dickens presents the death of Scrooge as the ultimate punishment for his greed and avarice, and the finality of death is depicted earlier in the novel through Marley's death and the death of Tiny Tim, for example. This ultimately moves Scrooge to transform completely.

Grade 7+ sample answer – Check the skills (page 79)

Points: The novel opens with the reference to Marley's death. Dickens wants the death to be understood as real. Scrooge's avarice is conveyed by a reference to how he saved money when arranging the funeral. This connection between the themes of money and death is continued throughout. The death of Tiny Tim forces Scrooge to accept responsibility for his actions.

Context: A literary connection to the death of Hamlet's father as another text that depends on the literal existence of ghosts.

Interpretation: I believe that the pivotal 'death' of Tiny Tim's arguably has a greatest impact on Scrooge than any other event.

ANSWERS

Grade 7+ sample answer – Now you try! (page 79)

AO1

- Avarice leads Joe and the other characters to greedy, criminal behaviour, 'You don't mean to say you took 'em down, rings and all, with him lying there?'
- As Scrooge's main weakness, avarice destroys his relationship with Belle and cuts him off from the rest of world as he is able to see only the importance of 'balancing your books'.
- Marley is punished for his avarice: 'I wear the chain I forged in life.'

AO2

- Dickens uses humour in this scene to depict avarice such as the hyperbolic statement 'I wouldn't give another sixpence, if I was to be boiled for not doing it.'
- The charwoman's rhetorical question, 'Why not?', suggests her unapologetic attitude towards her avaricious behaviour.
- Dickens uses structural repetition when his question to the charity collectors in Stave One, 'Are there no prisons?' comes back to haunt him in Stave Three as he sees the children Ignorance and Want.

AO3

- Dickens was angered by the Poor Law (1834) which led to the building of the workhouses, and the depiction of Scrooge's avarice and lack of compassion is a comment on wider Victorian society.
- Dickens presents Old Joe's shop in an area of London that 'reeked with crime, with filth, and misery' that shows how even in a rich city there are areas that have been devastated by poverty and avarice.

Practice questions – Question 6 (page 80)

AO1

- Scrooge is presented with the knowledge that Tiny Tim will die 'if these shadows remain unaltered', conveying the power Scrooge has over Tim's life and death.
- Scrooge's relationship with his own father as a child is very distant. Bob and Tim represent an ideal relationship: 'dreaded he might be taken from him'.
- Scrooge's redemption involves becoming a 'second father' to Tiny Tim.

AO2

- 'I see a vacant seat … and a crutch without an owner': Dickens uses imagery to suggest the poignancy of Tiny Tim's death.
- 'No, no! … Oh no…' Scrooge's repetition here reflects his strong emotions as the bond between Scrooge and Tim deepen.
- Dickens describes Scrooge's departure from this scene later in the Stave: he has his eye 'especially on Tiny Tim' as the final comment, conveying his new-found compassion for Tim.

AO3

- Tiny Tim's Christian message is repeated at the end of the novel and is a key motif.
- The idea to 'decrease the surplus population' was put forward by the nineteenth-century thinker Thomas Malthus, who suggested that poverty and overcrowding would be solved by the increased death rate among the poor.

Practice questions – Question 7 (page 81)

AO1

- The Cratchits have fun, 'Martha hid herself', and enjoy each other's company, despite their poverty, presenting a contrast with the solitary, but wealthy, Scrooge.
- The Cratchits represent how family can help you overcome hardship. Martha has had to work almost overnight on Christmas Eve and Tim has 'limbs supported by an iron frame' but they face those hardships together.
- All families in the novel are represented as loving, such as Belle's 'flushed and boisterous' children and Fred's 'musical family'. It is only Scrooge's immediate family that are distant and send him away to boarding school.

AO2

- Mrs Cratchit uses affectionate epithets, 'precious father' and 'my dear', to convey her love. Scrooge's transformation in Stave Five is similarly conveyed by the way he uses 'my dear', when addressing Fred's family servant.
- Hyperbole is used to express Fan's excessive happiness at the change in family circumstances, while hinting at Scrooge's lonely childhood: their father is 'so much kinder than he used to be, that home's like Heaven!'
- Scrooge's welcome back to Fred's family is described as 'wonderful unanimity'. The abstract noun conveys the sense of togetherness or 'one spirit'.

AO3

- Dickens had a complicated relationship with his parents and his own family as an adult, but he frequently presented the close and loving family as an ideal.
- Dickens despised the Victorian workhouses for their routine separation of parents and children as he understood the trauma and suffering this caused.